Cofounder AI

CLARENCE WOOTEN

Cofounder.AI

© 2025, Clarence Wooten

All rights reserved. This book or any portion thereof may not be reproduced or used in any manner whatsoever without the express written permission of the publisher except for the use of brief quotations in a book review.

Print ISBN: 979-8-35098-522-1
eBook ISBN: 979-8-35098-523-8

Contents

Acknowledgements 1

Introduction 3

1. The Cofounder Conundrum 15

2. The Founder's Playbook 33

3. Conceptualize (The Seed) 47

4. Launch! (The Grape Stage) 63

5. Iterate (Nailing Product-Market Fit) 77

6. Scale (A Grape, Grapefruit & Beyond) 91

7. Exit (Your Watermelon) 105

8. Seeing Around The Corner 117

Glossary 123

The AI Primer 135

Acknowledgements

"Great things in business are never done by one person; they're done by a team of people."

– Steve Jobs

Writing a book is much like building a startup—it's a collective effort driven by vision, collaboration, and trust. The vision for *CoFounder. AI* is my own, but, as with every startup I've been a part of, success is never a solo endeavor. It requires a team of stakeholders who believe in you and your vision—people willing to invest their time and energy, review drafts, offer suggestions, and challenge you to think differently, stay vulnerable, and keep it real.

To David Cassie and Hal Clifford, your expertise in the art of book crafting provided the wireframe I needed to transform an idea into a finished product. To my beta testers—David Jones, Mecca McDonald, and so many others—your honest feedback fueled the iterative process that refined and improved this work. I appreciate you.

To my family—Satin, Jordan, Avery, and Ohni—and my closest friends, you were the patient investors, offering me the runway and the motivation to bring this vision to life. You are my inspiration. To my parents, Clarence Sr. and Cecelia Wooten, I owe everything that I am today to the sacrifices you made for me, the self-confidence you instilled in me, and your unwavering love and support of me. I am truly blessed to be your son.

To Kellyn Yvonne Standley, your editorial insights sharpened this book's message, ensuring it reached its full potential. And finally, to you, the reader—thank you for embracing this work. It's early adopters like you, who make every step of this journey worthwhile.

My motto is: *learn, earn, and return.* This book is a reflection of all three. I hope you enjoy it.

Introduction

"AI is the ultimate force multiplier for startups, enabling them to accomplish in minutes what would have taken weeks or months."

– Eric Schmidt, Former CEO of Google

About This Book

Imagine building a billion-dollar startup... by yourself. Sounds impossible, right? Not anymore. Welcome to the age of AI-powered entrepreneurship.

CoFounder.AI isn't just a book—it's your launchpad into the future of startup building. Whether you're starting from scratch or well into your journey, this guide will show you how to harness AI throughout all phases of the company-building process, enabling you to do 10x more with 10x less. It's the ultimate bootstrapping tool, accelerating your journey across the Five Stages of Startup Success: **Conceptualize**, **Launch**, **Iterate**, **Scale**, and **Exit**.

AI won't build your startup for you—not yet—but once you master the strategies in this book, you'll see how AI becomes an accelerator that pushes you ahead of the curve.

The Power of AI in Startups

Picture this: It's 2 AM, you're knee-deep in market research, and your human cofounder is fast asleep. But your AI cofounder? It's wide awake, crunching numbers, generating product ideas, and even drafting your pitch deck. That's the power of AI in startups.

Throughout this book, you'll learn how to leverage AI at every stage:

- **Conceptualize:** Use AI for idea validation and deck creation (Chapter 3)
- **Launch:** Employ AI analytics for your minimal lovable product (MLP) (Chapter 4)
- **Iterate:** Harness AI for rapid prototyping and user feedback analysis (Chapter 5)
- **Scale:** Utilize AI for growth hacking and operational efficiency (Chapter 6)
- **Exit:** Apply AI for exit strategy planning and acquirer analysis (Chapter 7)

You'll also learn about the Reverse Liquidity Planning™ process (Chapter 7), a strategy to engineer your exit from day one.

AI Insight: Companies like Jasper.ai used AI to create marketing content, reaching a $1.5 billion valuation within 18 months. That's the kind of acceleration we're talking about.

I won't sugar-coat anything. The journey of any startup is daunting, but CoFounder.AI shows you how to turn AI into your personal copilot at every stage. The kicker? You might even realize you don't need that traditional cofounder after all. But if you do decide to bring on a human partner, this book will show you exactly how to find, vet, and partner with the right one.

And here's the reality: this isn't just about AI or cofounders. It's about the powerful synergy between them. Consider AI as the cofounder embedded in your journey—guiding, mentoring, and providing the structure, insight, and direction you need to stay focused.

This book will show you how to leverage AI through the five critical stages of startup success. You'll find strategies, tips, and, of course, AI tools tailored to each phase, helping you hit key milestones faster and more efficiently.

You'll also get an insider's view from my own journey and those of other founders. These stories aren't just about the big wins but about the stumbles, the setbacks, and the hard lessons learned along the way. Because let's be real: not every story ends with a perfect exit. But every story has lessons that can make your path smoother.

Now that you've got a glimpse of what's in store, it's time for a deeper dive into how we'll navigate this journey together—and why I'm the one guiding you through it.

From Baltimore Streets to Silicon Valley Exits

No one ever said being an entrepreneur was going to be easy. But then again, life itself isn't easy—a lesson I learned early on. Growing up in Walbrook Junction, one of Baltimore's most underserved neighborhoods, gave me a firsthand education in the harsh realities of survival. I wasn't just reading about grit, I was living it. By fifth grade, I had dodged stick-up kids more times than I could count. And then one day, my luck ran out—I was held at gunpoint for my sneakers.

For entrepreneurs, our drive often comes from those early, pivotal struggles. Those streets not only battle-tested me, but surviving them gave me a combination of grit and gratitude that has helped me keep things in perspective throughout the ups and downs. Now, most people won't face the same threats I did, but make no mistake—your startup journey will have its own "do or die" moments.

My humble beginnings taught me one thing above all else: when you don't have a network or a mentor to fall back on, you rely on grit. And let me tell you, that grit carried me from those Baltimore streets to becoming the only Black American tech entrepreneur to have founded, scaled, and led two internet startups to successful acquisitions by publicly traded companies.

I don't take any pride in being "the only." That's why I wrote this book—to give you the real, hard-hitting truth; coupled with a playbook to get you not just from zero to one, but from zero to done.

Entrepreneurship has always been in my DNA, but my path certainly hasn't been easy. Along the way, I made plenty of mistakes, wasted time, and took more than my share of detours. There's an old Chinese proverb: "Experience teaches slowly, at the cost of mistakes." I learned that the hard way, but every stumble helped me refine the approach that I'm sharing with you.

For new entrepreneurs, the uncertainty can be paralyzing. You don't know what you don't know, and that's the toughest part. How do I take the first step? Should I go solo or bring on a cofounder? Is my idea even fundable? And if so, should I bootstrap or chase venture capital? How do I find investors when I don't have a built-in network, and perhaps the biggest question of all: How do I get traction without capital?

Every founder has grappled with these questions. And while the answers are never simple, one thing is clear—there's nothing more exhilarating, or more terrifying, than turning your vision into reality. If you know deep down that you're meant to be an entrepreneur, then despite the uncertainties, as Nike says: *Just Do It*. Let this book guide you, accelerating your path to success.

I wrote this to help you avoid the same mistakes I made. To save you from wasting time in dead ends and help you stay focused on the right things, right from the start. While my entrepreneurial journey is far from over, my focus has broadened. These days, I'm dedicated to helping founders like you build companies that don't just scale but solve real-world problems and enrich lives.

From Serial Entrepreneur to Moonshot Maker

Today, I'm an Executive and Entrepreneur in Residence at Alphabet's "moonshot factory," X—also known as Google [X], not to be confused with the company formerly known as Twitter. Here, I hunt for opportunities to create and leverage radical new technologies to solve some of the World's biggest and hardest problems creating the foundation for large enduring businesses.

I've seen firsthand what AI can do, and I believe its impact will go far beyond 10x. Just imagine what it can do for your startup. I hope this book becomes your roadmap, showing you how to harness AI to bring your vision to life and, perhaps, change the world along the way.

You'll learn from my experiences, including:

- The **ImageCafe** story and the lessons of "cofounder equity remorse" (Chapter 1)
- The **Groupsite** journey from high-growth startup to lifestyle business (Chapter 6)
- The **Progressly** tale of misaligned cofounders and its impact on scaling (Chapter 5)

I didn't grow up surrounded by successful entrepreneurs, but I devoured their stories. I read about Bill Gates, *Reginald Lewis*,[1] and others who built empires from nothing. What stuck with me? The common thread—every one of them faced near-death experiences for their companies. It wasn't talent alone that saved them; it was their refusal to quit, their belief in themselves when no one else would, and their ability to apply leverage.

Take Airbnb. Brian Chesky and Joe Gebbia were just two guys struggling to pay rent in San Francisco. Their idea—renting out air mattresses to conference attendees—sounded borderline absurd. But it worked. That humble, half-crazy idea turned into a multi-billion-dollar company that disrupted an entire industry. Their story, like so many others, is a reminder that greatness often starts from the most unexpected places.

Insights to Guide Your Entrepreneurial Journey

Before embarking on your journey toward greatness, here are a few valuable insights that will serve you well:

1. **The joy is in the journey, not the destination.** When you're too focused on the endgame, you miss the wins along the way. Building a company is a marathon, not a sprint. You better love the process, or you're going to burn out fast.

2. **Most entrepreneurs overestimate what they can accomplish in a year and grossly underestimate what they can achieve in ten.**

---

1. **Reginald F. Lewis** (1942–1993) was a trailblazing African American entrepreneur, lawyer, and philanthropist, best known for being the first Black American to build a billion-dollar company through a leveraged buyout.

That's why you have to think long-term—five, ten years ahead. Which only works if you are truly passionate about your mission.

3. **With or without AI, business is a team sport.** One of the most critical things you control is who you build your company with. Your first hires set the tone for your startup's culture. A-players hire A+ players, people who are smarter than they are. B-players, on the other hand, hire C-players. They hire out of insecurity, and that's the death knell for any startup. In my experience, the DNA of your first ten hires will define your company for years to come.

4. **The most successful entrepreneurs don't just grind; they leverage other people's time and money to scale.** So as you build, your ability to apply leverage will determine just how far and how fast you can go.

For decades, venture capital has been the primary tool for applying leverage. But today, we have something even more powerful—artificial intelligence (AI). You've probably heard AI's potential to change every industry, and in this book, I'll show you how to use it as the ultimate bootstrapping tool as you build your startup. If leveraged properly, it will significantly reduce the amount of money you need to raise.

Small Businesses vs. High-Growth Startups

I'll cut to the chase: if your dream is to open a quaint coffee shop and run it for the next 25 years, this book probably isn't for you. But if you're thinking, "How can I turn that coffee shop into the next Starbucks?"—keep reading.

Small business owners run small businesses while startup founders are wired to think in terms of scale. The U.S. Government's Small Business Administration (SBA) defines a Small Business as a company with 500 employees or less. So technically, startups in their early stages are small businesses. The difference is in their intent.

The goal of a startup is not to remain a startup—it's to grow quickly into a large enterprise. While small business owners often focus on steady, sustainable growth, primarily serving local communities. Startup founders aim to disrupt markets, redefine industries, and ultimately make waves on a global scale. We don't just want to be our own boss—we want to build something transformative.

I know the difference in mindsets well. I grew up in a family of small business owners. My parents, without college degrees, chose self-employment to avoid underemployment. Their focus? Stability, full ownership, and generating enough income to support the family. But for startup entrepreneurs, stability isn't the goal—scale is. We're not interested in maintaining the status quo; we're here to shift it.

Here's how I think of it: a small business is like a grape. It's contained, small, and its growth is limited by the vision of its owner. Startup founders aim to turn that grape into a watermelon, and we do it by using leverage—other people's time, money, and resources—by using equity as currency. Sure, your ownership percentage will shrink, but the value of your company will grow exponentially.

Quick Action: Ask yourself: Do you want to own 100% of a grape or 20% of a watermelon? Your answer defines your entrepreneurial path.

Startup founders dream of introducing innovative products that change the game. We prioritize growth over short-term profits, chasing equity funding from angel investors and venture capitalists (VCs) to grab market share as fast as we can. The idea is simple: your startup itself is the asset, and with every new customer, your equity value climbs. It's not about making profits today—it's about creating value tomorrow. And when we achieve that exponential growth, the reward comes in the form of a lucrative exit, whether through acquisition or going public. And if you're anything like me, once you've tasted success, you'll keep looking for your next venture. So when you get there, I want to hear all about it.

The Future is Now: Your AI Cofounder Awaits

If the title of this book didn't already give it away, we're heading into a new era—the era of the AI cofounder. Before you can fully appreciate what that means, I want you to understand the value a human cofounder brings.

Cofounders aren't always essential, but the right one can be transformative. A cofounder with complementary skills, shared passion, and the persistence to grind through the rough patches can be the difference between success and failure. But make no mistake: a bad cofounder can sink your company just as quickly. A "cofounder divorce" can be a startup killer. In Chapter 1, I'll walk you through what I call the "Cofounder Conundrum"—how to find the right partner and, just as importantly, how to vet them.

Finally, as we explore in Chapter 8, we're entering an era where AI isn't just a tool—it's becoming a digital species. From multimodal AI that can interpret visual and auditory cues to AI with an *action quotient (AQ)*,[2] the possibilities are expanding rapidly.

Sam Altman of OpenAI predicts the world's first one-person, billion-dollar company is just around the corner, powered by AI. Why not make it yours?

---

2. **Action quotient (AQ)** refers to an individual's or organization's ability to take effective action in real-time, especially in response to complex situations or decision-making environments.

Final Quick Action: Before you turn the page, take a moment to write down your wildest startup dream. No holds barred. Now, let's make it happen—with a little help from AI.

Ready to meet your new cofounder? Let's dive in.

Before we get started, know that this isn't just another handbook on scaling a company by chasing venture capital or angel investors. Sure, we'll cover that, but the real focus here is on showing you how AI can be the ultimate bootstrapping tool. From concept to exit, AI is going to become your biggest ally in maximizing what you can build with the resources you have.

Every phase of the startup journey—whether you're just sketching out ideas or eyeing a *liquidity event*[3]—is covered. More importantly, you'll learn how to combine capital with AI to open up multiple exit opportunities as your business scales.

And here's the kicker: *CoFounder.AI* isn't static. It's a constantly updating platform powered by its own Large Language Model (LLM). Which means it's always evolving, adding new AI tools and resources as they become available. Now, you could jump ahead and dive right into the platform by visiting CoFounder.AI or by scanning the QR code below, but I recommend you stick around and read a little more—there will be plenty of opportunities throughout the book.

Besides, the foundation of knowledge you'll gain from these pages will help you unlock the true potential of the AI resources waiting for you in the platform's community. If you are new to startup entrepreneurship, financial terminology, or AI, I recommend that you start by reading **How Startup**

---

3. **Liquidity event:** A liquidity event is a financial transaction that allows investors and/or employees in a privately held company to cash out some or all of their ownership shares.

Finance Works and **The AI Primer**—both available in the glossary at the end of this book.

Note: Whenever you see this AI icon 🦙 in these pages, it's your signal that there's something waiting for you in the *CoFounder.AI* platform community—specific AI tools, prompts and workflows designed to dramatically speed up your task.

CHAPTER 1

The Cofounder Conundrum

"The cofounder relationship is like a marriage. It requires trust, communication, and a shared vision for the future."

—Larry Page, Cofounder of Google

The ImageCafe Story: A Lesson in Cofounder Equity Remorse

Picture this: It's 1998. DVDs are the hot new thing, Google just launched, and most people are still figuring out what this "internet" thing is all about. Meanwhile, my friend Andre and I are about to embark on a wild, life-changing ride that will teach us some hard lessons about the startup world.

From Agency to Product: The Birth of ImageCafe

Together, Andre and I were running a small interactive agency called Metamorphosis Studios, but we had bigger dreams. We wanted to build something that would "make money while we sleep." After brainstorming many product ideas and building prototypes for them, we landed on an idea that seems obvious now: What if we could productize our web design skills?

That's how ImageCafe was born. Our vision: Create an online superstore packed with customizable website templates for small business owners. Remember, this was before Wix, Shopify, or WordPress. Most small businesses had two options for getting online:

1. Let your tech-savvy nephew build you a site that looked like it was designed by... well, your nephew.
2. Shell out big bucks to a design agency.

We saw an opportunity to disrupt this market by offering "customizable website masters." Which sounded more sophisticated than templates. Our slogan, "Look like the Fortune 500, for under $500." Spoiler alert: We were right. But running a product business is a different beast than running a service agency. Suddenly, we needed investor cash to give us runway, and while we were no strangers to bootstrapping, we were a little naïve about how far scrappiness alone could take us.

The Hustle: From Idea to Investment

As CEO, I dove headfirst into the fundraising hustle. I literally went from Silicon Valley to *Silicon Alley*,[4] pitching our vision to anyone who would listen. Investors liked what they saw, and soon, we were off to the races.

But here's where things got tricky. While I was crisscrossing the country, managing operations, and overseeing staff at our office in Maryland, Andre worked remotely from Florida. Furthermore, he felt strongly that ImageCafe

---

4. **Silicon Alley** refers to the technology hub in New York City, particularly concentrated in areas like Manhattan and Brooklyn.

should also include personal website templates. I disagreed. I insisted that we remain focused on serving small businesses.

Ultimately, we stayed the course, but as time went on, Andre's desire to remain in Florida and our conflicting visions started to drive a wedge between us.

The Breaking Point

A pivotal turning point for the company came when we secured representation from Wilson, Sonsini, Goodrich, and Rosati (WSGR), a powerhouse law firm in Silicon Valley. This was huge—WSGR had direct lines to top VCs and represented Internet giants including Yahoo and Netscape. Their backing gave us credibility, opened doors, and moved us closer to raising our $3 million Series A. But with every step forward, the tension between Andre and I only grew worse.

Deciding to remain in Florida and not move back to Maryland, Andre dropped a bombshell: "Let's keep it simple—split the $3 million once the round closes. I'll take $1.5 million and build a version of ImageCafe focused on Personal Websites, while you continue to run ImageCafe from Maryland."

I was floored. We were less than a month away from closing our Series A and we were not aligned. I was frustrated by Andre's unwillingness to move back to Maryland to assist with operations. Andre was frustrated by my unwillingness to expand the vision. I worried that our rift and Andre's proposed departure would spook the investors—it almost did. ImageCafe couldn't sustain the imbalance any longer. We were moving in different directions and our staff could feel it.

The Buyout: A Bittersweet Solution

Long story short, WSGR suggested that the company use a promissory note to buy Andre out. We structured a deal that included a promissory note, plus an ongoing equity percentage in the company that we could agree on. The entire process and Andre's departure delayed our Series A. This turned out to be a blessing. A few months later, Network Solutions offered $23 million to acquire ImageCafe. We accepted the offer.

The Startup Standard: Vest From Day One

In the end it was a big win for everyone involved. However, if I could go back, I'd do things differently. The big lesson? All founders should vest their equity from day one. This means stock gets released over time, typically three to four years. If someone leaves early, they don't walk away with a chunk of the company they didn't fully earn.

Prior to structuring the buyout deal with Andre, I was feeling "cofounder equity remorse," which could have been avoided had we known about *vesting*[5] at the start. Thankfully it all worked out. Andre and I remain close, and we continue to do business together today. Success has a way of making everyone happy.

Quick Action: Before reading on, jot down what you think are the three most important qualities in a cofounder. We'll revisit this later.

The Cofounder Checklist: Questions to Ask Before You Leap

The story of *ImageCafe* isn't unique—plenty of founders have experienced cofounder equity remorse. But that doesn't mean having a cofounder is a bad idea. In fact, in many situations, a cofounder is exactly what you need to take your startup to the next level.

---

5. **Vesting** is the process where an employee gradually earns ownership of benefits or stock options provided by their employer over time.

The challenge lies in finding *the right* cofounder, not just any cofounder. It's a bit like dating—you don't want to rush into it without asking the tough questions first. Here is a checklist:

1. **Vision and Mission Alignment**

    ◦ Where do you see this company in five years? Ten years?

    ◦ Why are you passionate about solving this problem?

    ◦ What's your personal endgame here—financial success, social impact, or something else?

2. **Values and Culture Fit**

    ◦ What core values should guide our company?

    ◦ How do you balance profit with social responsibility?

    ◦ What's your take on diversity and inclusion in building our team?

3. **Work Ethic and Commitment**

    ◦ How many hours a week are you ready to put into this?

    ◦ What does work-life balance mean to you?

    ◦ Can you stick it out through the tough times?

4. **Risk Tolerance and Decision Making**

    ◦ How do you handle uncertainty?

    ◦ What's your approach to making decisions under pressure?

    ◦ Are you open to pivoting if the market tells us we're off track?

5. **Roles and Responsibilities**
    - What's your superpower—where do you shine?
    - How should we divide responsibilities?
    - How do we resolve disagreements when we clash?

6. **Funding and Growth**
    - Bootstrapping or VC funding—where do you stand?
    - What are your thoughts on equity division?
    - Fast scaling or steady growth—which camp are you in?

7. **Exit Strategy**
    - Are you thinking acquisition, IPO, or building a legacy company?
    - What's your timeline for an exit, if any?

8. **Communication and Feedback**
    - How do you prefer to hash out conflicts?
    - How do you handle giving and receiving feedback?
    - How often should we check in on each other's performance?

AI-Powered Tip: Use the CoFounder.AI platform to generate personalized cofounder compatibility questions based on your background, skills and initial startup idea. It's like having a seasoned startup advisor at your disposal.

The Cofounder Marriage: For Better or Worse

Choosing a cofounder is a lot like getting married. You're in it for the long haul, through the late nights, the pivots, and the rollercoaster of startup life. Here's how to make sure your "business marriage" doesn't end in a messy divorce. Remember, you're not just looking for a yes-person. You want someone whose strengths complement yours. The goal is synergy—where 1 + 1 = more than 2.

Shared Sacrifice and Commitment

Both of you need to be all in. If one person is pulling all-nighters while the other is Netflix and chilling, resentment will build faster than your user base.

Real Talk: Have the tough conversations early. How will this impact your personal life? If you've got a partner or kids, they need to be on board too. Trust me, as a dad building startups, I had to find a balance.

I wasn't going to let being an entrepreneur turn me into an absentee father. That meant saying "no" to a lot of opportunities that might have been good for my business—conferences, networking events, etc.—if they conflicted with my time with my daughters. As a divorced dad with 50/50 joint custody, my time was their time, and trust me, my daughters made sure I remembered that when I needed a reminder. Sure, it might've slowed my business progress a bit, but it's a decision I'll never regret.

As I saw it, you only get 18 years to raise your kids, and those years shape who they become and what kind of relationship you'll have with them for the rest of your life. To me, that was more important than any company I could build. My daughters, Jordan and Avery, are and always will be the best two startups I'll ever create. Today, I am blessed to say, they are thriving.

Cofounder Compatibility

Building a strong cofounder relationship is about more than just shared goals; it's about creating a foundation of complementary strengths, open communication, and trust. Here are some things to remember:

Complementary Personalities

You don't need to be twins. In fact, it's better if you're not. An introvert paired with an extrovert can be a killer combo. The key is finding someone who fills in your gaps.

Open Communication and Trust

No secrets, no BS. You need to be able to disagree without things falling apart. Check your ego at the door and trust that your cofounder's got valuable insights too.

Conflict Management 101

Spoiler alert: You're going to fight. The trick isn't avoiding conflict—it's knowing how to handle it. Don't let small issues fester into deal-breakers.

Making Tough Decisions

Stuck at a crossroads? Try this: Rate how much you care about the decision on a scale of one to ten. If your cofounder's a nine and you're a five, consider deferring to them. Just make sure you're both honest—if everything's a ten, you're in for a rough ride.

Planning for Dissolution

Hope for the best, plan for the worst. Have a clear breakup strategy for if (when) things go south. Trust me, future you will thank present you for this foresight.

A successful cofounder marriage: Chipotle Mexican Grill

If you're curious about what a successful cofounder relationship looks like, the story of Steve Ells and Monty Moran from Chipotle Mexican Grill serves as an inspiring example.

> Steve Ells, a Culinary Institute of America graduate, understood the typical goals of most fast-food chains: deliver a greasy burger, fries, or maybe a fried chicken sandwich as quickly as possible—ideally without the customer even needing to leave their car. But Ells wondered, did it really have to be that way?
>
> He believed there had to be a way to provide customers with the speed and efficiency they expected without compromising on quality. His vision was to replace frozen patties, deep fryers, and shake machines with fresh, high-quality ingredients, served hot and customized to each customer's preference. However, there was a significant obstacle: Ells wasn't a businessperson. He had no idea how to turn his culinary dream into a successful reality.
>
> This is where his former culinary professor, Monty Moran, came into the picture. Moran recognized the potential in Ells's idea and, when approached, eagerly embraced the opportunity to form a partnership.
>
> This partnership exemplifies one of the key elements of a successful cofounder relationship—complementary skills. Ells brought innovation and culinary expertise to the table, while Moran contributed his business acumen, including the ability to secure funding and prime real estate. Their partnership gave them a strategic advantage, as they each leaned into their strengths and trusted the other to compensate for their weaknesses.

Their journey wasn't without challenges. The cofounders had their share of disagreements, but they maintained honest and open communication, never allowing emotions to cloud their judgment about what was best for the business. They prioritized long-term success over personal pride. In moments of conflict, they likely asked themselves, "Would you rather be successful, or would you rather be right?"

Chipotle flourished because its cofounders shared a common vision and values. Their unwavering commitment to these principles allowed the company to stand out in the crowded fast-food market. They offered something unique: fresh, high-quality ingredients served quickly and profitably.

The success of Chipotle is a powerful example of how the right cofounder can be the catalyst that propels a brilliant vision into a thriving reality.

What Happens When You Choose the Wrong Cofounder?

What happens if you're not as fortunate as Ells and Moran when it comes to choosing a cofounder? You wouldn't be the first to make that mistake, and you certainly won't be the last.

Choosing the wrong cofounder can lead to significant challenges that may slow your progress, but it doesn't have to spell the end of your business. Yes, it can be emotionally draining. Stress and anxiety are part of any startup journey, but these feelings are amplified when you're constantly at odds with your business partner.

In a traditional work environment, two feuding employees can disrupt their immediate surroundings. But when two founders are at war, it can bring the entire company down. Employees quickly lose motivation when they're caught in the crossfire between leaders who can't agree on even the most basic decisions. Just like children in a troubled marriage, they suffer from the tension. Morale plummets, and the company's public image may take a hit. Until the relationship is repaired, recovery is nearly impossible.

A toxic cofounder relationship often creates a chaotic workplace where arguments take center stage, draining valuable time and energy. This results in lost productivity, missed opportunities, and wasted resources. Worse still, decision paralysis sets in when you and your cofounder can't agree on much of anything. One way to break this deadlock is simple: compromise. If you're facing a list of ten disagreements, give your cofounder five and take five yourself. Don't let deadlock strangle the momentum of your business.

However, if it becomes clear that you can't resolve your differences, a "startup divorce" may be the only viable option. Unfortunately, if you didn't begin with the right agreements—or even if you did—this can lead to messy legal battles over equity, intellectual property, company assets, and more. In the end, both parties often emerge with lasting scars. It's an outcome everyone hopes to avoid, but one that underscores the importance of building a strong foundation from the start.

When Cofounder Relationships Go Sour: The OpenAI Saga

Not every cofounder story has a happy ending. Case in point: Elon Musk and Sam Altman of OpenAI.

> *Elon Musk and Sam Altman were both key figures in the early development of OpenAI, an organization founded in 2015 with the mission of advancing artificial intelligence in a safe and beneficial*

way. However, tensions eventually arose between Musk and the leadership at OpenAI, including Altman, leading to Musk's departure from the company's board in 2018.

Elon Musk's departure from OpenAI stemmed from a combination of factors, primarily disagreements over the company's direction and control.

- **Disagreement on Progress and Strategy**: Musk believed that OpenAI was falling significantly behind Google in AI development and proposed taking control of the company himself. This proposal was rejected by OpenAI's other founders, leading to conflict.

- **Conflict Over Funding and Control**: As OpenAI sought to transition to a for-profit structure to secure more resources for AI research, disagreements arose regarding the level of control Musk would have in the new entity. He wanted majority equity, initial board control, and the position of CEO, while OpenAI's founders sought a more distributed control structure.

- **Financial Commitments**: During these negotiations, Musk reportedly withheld funding he had previously pledged to OpenAI, creating further tension and contributing to the breakdown of the relationship.

Ultimately, these conflicts led to Musk leaving OpenAI in 2018, with both sides expressing support for each other's future endeavors. While the specifics of the conversations and negotiations remain somewhat private, it's clear that differences in vision and control were central to the split. In the years since Musk's departure from the board, Musk and Altman have at times praised each other's work.

However, since OpenAI's release of ChatGPT and rapid ensuing growth, Musk has repeatedly criticized OpenAI's ChatGPT chatbot as "woke" and launched a rival chatbot called Grok. Since then, Musk has filed a lawsuit accusing OpenAI and its chief executive, Sam Altman, of betraying its foundational mission by putting the pursuit of profit ahead of the benefit of humanity.

The saga continues.

Necessary Cofounder Agreements: Protecting Your Startup's Future

Remember the ImageCafe story? That taught me the hard way how crucial well-structured cofounder agreements are. Consider these elements when structuring your agreements:

1. **Equity Split Agreement**

    Decide how to divide the pie—options include:

    - **Equal Split:** Everyone gets the same slice.
    - **Unequal Split:** Based on experience, investment, or expected contribution.

    Tip: Include *Contribution Milestones*[6] for future resources or work.

2. **Vesting Schedule**

    Protect your startup with a typical 4-year vesting schedule with a 1-year cliff. This means:

---

6. **Contribution milestones** are specific, measurable targets that track individual or team progress toward key deliverables or goals in a project, ensuring accountability and alignment with overall objectives.

- No equity until after year one (the "cliff")
- A quarter (25%) vests at year one, then monthly or quarterly for the next three years

Consider acceleration clauses for acquisitions or terminations without cause.

3. **Roles and Responsibilities**

   Clearly define who does what. Include clauses for role changes or resignations.

4. **Founder Buyback Rights (Reverse Vesting)**

   Allow the company to buy back unvested shares if a founder leaves early. Specify conditions and pricing.

5. **IP Assignment and Ownership**

   Ensure all intellectual property created for the startup belongs to the company, not individuals.

6. **Non-Compete and Non-Solicitation Clauses**

   Prevent cofounders from immediately competing or poaching after leaving. Keep these reasonable and enforceable.

7. **Future Funding and Dilution**

   Agree on how future funding rounds will impact ownership. Consider preemptive rights for founders to maintain their percentage.

8. **Exit Strategy and Equity Liquidity**

   Outline scenarios for acquisitions, mergers, or IPOs. Include liquidation preferences and rights of first refusal for share sales.

9. **Dispute Resolution**

    Set up a process for resolving conflicts, including mediation or arbitration clauses. Have a plan for breaking deadlocks on major decisions.

10. **Termination and Departure**

    Specify conditions for founder removal and what happens to equity upon departure.

Remember, these agreements are about fairness and protecting relationships as much as they are about legalities. They provide a framework for handling future scenarios that may arise in your startup's journey.

AI Boost: Use AI-powered legal tech tools to draft initial versions of these agreements. They can provide templates based on industry standards and your specific inputs. But always have a startup-specialized lawyer review the final documents. For additional resources, the renowned tech law firm Cooley offers free startup documents at Cooley GO. Learn more at Cofounder.AI.

The Bottom Line: Choose Wisely, But Don't Go It Alone

Whether you opt for a human cofounder, an AI assistant, or some hybrid approach, the key is to build a support system that amplifies your strengths and shores up your weaknesses.

The journey of building a startup is a marathon, not a sprint. Choose your running mate wisely, be it flesh and blood or ones and zeros.

Remember, ideas alone aren't worth much until they're executed. Many founders mistakenly believe that having the idea makes them the de facto CEO, or that it gives them more say in the direction of the company. But that's not how it works. I often tell founders, "An idea is like having apples. Building a great startup is about turning those apples into the best apple pie. That requires more than just the fruit—you need the oven, the ingredients, and most importantly, the right talent."

While AI is rewriting what it means to have a cofounder, there are a few things you need to keep in mind. AI algorithms have their biases—this isn't some perfect, impartial machine. I dive deeper into these in The AI Primer at the end of the book, feel free to flip forward if you are interested. As AI continues to weave itself into the startup ecosystem, you'll get a clearer sense of how these systems operate and how to tweak them to fit your goals.

For now, understand that AI complements, but doesn't replace, human intuition. Creativity, leadership, and gut instinct remain the cornerstone of what makes founders successful.

Now, AI might handle a lot of the heavy lifting, but it's not a total replacement. It can't offer emotional support (at least, not yet) and won't fully share your vision for the business. Those human qualities are still crucial for long-term success. But AI is one hell of an accelerant on your journey.

So, if you decide to bring on a human cofounder, great—just don't forget to keep hitting that Easy Button as you build your startup. AI is improving by the day, and the dream of a "One Person Billion-Dollar Startup" is getting closer with every step forward.

Whenever you see this AI icon in these pages, it's your signal that there's something waiting for you in the *CoFounder.AI* platform community—specific tools, prompts and workflows designed to dramatically speed up your task.

By focusing on the bigger picture and asking the right questions upfront, you'll get a clear sense of the type of cofounder that works best for you.

Final Quick Action: Revisit the three qualities you wrote down at the beginning of this chapter. How many of these can be fulfilled by AI? How many require a human touch? Your answers might just guide your next big decision. Learn more at Cofounder.AI.

CHAPTER 2

The Founder's Playbook

"AI as a co-pilot in a startup is like having a seasoned mentor and a tireless assistant rolled into one—constantly optimizing decisions, accelerating growth, and empowering founders to focus on the vision rather than the grind."

— Clarence Wooten, Author, CoFounder.AI

This chapter lays out the roadmap—the core playbook that this entire book is built upon: *The Five Stages of Startup Success*. Understanding this framework is the key to building a startup with billion dollar potential. I crafted this playbook back in 2010 when I realized I'd become a go-to mentor for many young tech founders.

What started as casual advice evolved into a blog post on my personal site, *ClarenceWooten.com*, where I began directing new founders, since I was giving out the same advice on repeat. Over time, I've fine-tuned and expanded it with fresh lessons and insights—which continue to evolve, even as I write this book.

But before we dive into the details of the playbook, we need to address two fundamental concepts that will shape your mindset as a founder: *ownership* and *control*.

Mindset Shift #1: You're a Shareholder First

Here's a mind-bender for you: As a founder, you're not just the visionary behind your startup—you're its first investor. Even if all you've invested is time and brain power, congratulations! You're a shareholder. This isn't just semantics; it's a fundamental shift in how you approach your business.

I learned this lesson the hard way. In my early days, I was so focused on being "the CEO" that I forgot about the bigger picture. But here's the truth: to build something truly scalable, you need to think like a shareholder, not just a founder.

Remember when I talked about turning grapes into watermelons? This is where that comes into play. As you bring in outside capital and talent, your ownership percentage will shrink, but the overall value of your company (and your shares) will grow exponentially. It's simple math: would you rather own 100% of a grape or 20% of a watermelon?

My father used to say, "Clarence, always make sure you own at least 51% of your business." His reasoning was simple—51% meant control. And in the world of small business, that advice holds up. But it's a small business mindset, not a startup mindset.

Once I grasped the concept of leverage, I realized something: almost no founders who've built companies of significant scale own more than 10-20% at the time of exit. Look at Mark Zuckerberg—he owns just 13.6% of Facebook. Jeff Bezos, once the richest man in the world, owns less than 9% of Amazon.

These founders understood something crucial: they were shareholders first, and in many cases, as their companies grew, their roles evolved. They focused on what was best for the business, even if that meant shifting their personal involvement. As a shareholder first, what's best for the business is almost always what's best for you.

Mindset Shift #2: Control Isn't About 51%

Now, here's where it gets interesting. When no one shareholder holds a majority stake, maintaining control over your startup becomes more about who has influence over the board of directors than about ownership percentages.

Think of your board as the steering wheel of your startup. Even if you don't own more than 51%, you can keep control by steering the decisions that come from the boardroom. It's all about votes and influence.

It's also important to know that boards aren't formed by accident. They come together when founders raise money from venture capital investors. When capital is invested, the lead investor will negotiate for a board seat. The initial board is usually comprised of the founder/ceo, the lead investor and an independent board director that the founder and investor can agree on

Here's a quick breakdown:

1. **The Board's Role:** They handle the big stuff—hiring or firing the CEO, signing off on company strategy, and approving fundraising rounds.
2. **Board Composition:** You've got founders, investors, and independent members.
3. **How Control Works:** It's all about votes and alliances. If you can influence who sits on the board, you effectively maintain control.

4. **Maintaining Control with Less Ownership:** Focus on structuring board control agreements, establishing supermajority voting requirements for major decisions, and negotiating founder-friendly terms.

Now that we've shifted your mindset, let's dive into the playbook itself—the Five Stages of Startup Success. This isn't just theory; it's the battle-tested roadmap I've used and refined over decades in the startup trenches. First, let's start with a case study that exemplifies how the mindset shift ultimately created a billionaire.

The Evolution of Reid Hoffman's Role at LinkedIn: A Masterclass in Startup Leadership

Picture this: It's 2002, and Reid Hoffman is about to launch LinkedIn. Fresh off his PayPal success, he's got the Midas touch. It turns out, Hoffman's real superpower isn't just starting companies, it's knowing when to pass the baton.

Hoffman's LinkedIn journey is like a three-act play, each act showcasing a different leadership role:

1. Founder and CEO (2002 - 2007)

Hoffman launched LinkedIn in 2002, taking the reins as CEO during its formative years. With his entrepreneurial experience—fresh off the success of PayPal—he spearheaded the company's early development. Securing funding, building a team, and growing a user base were his forte. But as LinkedIn began to scale, Hoffman faced a critical realization: the skills needed to start a company aren't the same as those required to run a large, complex organization. He knew LinkedIn would need a different kind of leadership to reach its full potential.

2. The Shift to Executive Chairman (2007 - 2016)

As LinkedIn accelerated in growth, Hoffman made a pivotal move in 2007—he stepped down as CEO and brought in Dan Nye, an experienced operator. Shifting to the role of Executive Chairman, Hoffman focused on the high-level vision and long-term strategy, leaving the operational grind to Nye. This move allowed him to steer the ship without being bogged down by day-to-day decisions, but still staying deeply involved in product development and the company's overall direction.

3. Bringing in Jeff Weiner (2009)

In 2009, Hoffman's strategic foresight shone again when he tapped Jeff Weiner, a former Yahoo executive, to take over as CEO. Weiner had the operational expertise LinkedIn needed at a critical moment—scaling up, monetizing the platform, and preparing for its IPO. Under Weiner's leadership, LinkedIn executed a flawless public offering in 2011, cementing its place as a global powerhouse. Hoffman's willingness to hand over the reins wasn't a relinquishing of control, but a savvy recognition of what LinkedIn needed to thrive.

4. Mentorship and Strategic Vision (2016 and Beyond)

Even after LinkedIn's monumental $26.2 billion acquisition by Microsoft in 2016, Hoffman didn't fade into the background. He remained on the board, offering guidance while continuing to mentor startups through Greylock Partners. His journey from CEO to Executive Chairman, and eventually to board member and investor, speaks volumes about his grasp of what truly matters—being a shareholder and visionary, rather than clinging to a title.

Hoffman's story is a powerful reminder for founders: success isn't about holding onto control for control's sake. It's about recognizing when your company needs a different type of leadership and being strategic enough to make that shift. Reid Hoffman's journey epitomizes the mindset required to turn a grape into a watermelon. The sale of LinkedIn to Microsoft made Reid a billionaire.

The Five Stages of Startup Success (Chapter Outline)

Stage 1: Conceptualize *(Chapter 3)*

This is where you turn your idea into something real. You'll validate your concept, create a pitch deck, and maybe even develop a prototype. It's about laying the groundwork for everything that follows.

- **Identify** a problem and devise a solution.
- **Validate** that your solution and the solution is technically feasible and there is a *significant market* willing and able to pay for it.
- **Create** a killer pitch deck with visuals and a narrative you can share with potential stakeholders.
- **Engage** with key stakeholders—potential customers, team members, and investors. See how they respond to your proposed solution.
- **Develop** a mockup, prototype, or alpha version of your product.
- **Establish** your corporate structure (founders' stock, stock option plan, etc.).
- **Raise** pre-seed capital (friends and family round) to fuel your startup through the launch phase.

AI Tool Alert: Use AI as your market research tool to validate your idea faster than ever. Use the CoFounder.AI platform to get started.

Stage 2: Launch *(Chapter 4)*

Time to introduce your baby to the world. But remember, no business plan survives first contact with customers. This stage is all about getting real-world feedback and being ready to pivot if needed.

- **Develop** your product based on feedback from potential customers (private beta)
  - Establish minimal feature set
  - Establish product usage and sales metrics
  - Establish a go-to-market strategy
- **Recruit** a board of advisors (brain trust) and incentivize them with stock options to open doors for you.
- **Leverage** early pre-launch hype to raise enough capital (Seed investment) to sustain operation for 12-18 months—you'll need a post-launch runway to iterate.
- **Remain** in private beta until you have a MLP (Minimal Lovable Product).
- **Plan** and coordinate your official go-to-market (GTM) strategy now that your minimal lovable product (MLP) is ready for primetime (PR, launch event, press tour, etc).
- **Launch** publicly with as much publicity as you can muster (news, blog posts, etc.)—or launch quietly with no initial publicity until you can demonstrate consistent sales success and customer retention (aka product-market fit).

AI Hack: Leverage AI for customer feedback analysis. It can spot trends and insights humans might miss. Learn more at Cofounder.AI.

Stage 3: Iterate *(Chapter 5)*

This is where the real work begins. You'll refine your product based on user feedback, tweaking and improving until you hit that sweet spot of product-market fit.

1. **Monitor** initial product and sales metrics in the weeks following the launch.
2. **Refine** product based on feedback from initial customers.
   - Improve existing features making them more user-friendly.
   - Add secondary feature set.
3. **Modify** your product and sales strategy where necessary.
4. **Repeat** steps 1-3 until you can demonstrate consistent sales success and customer retention (aka, product-market fit).

AI Superpower: Use AI-driven A/B testing tools to iterate faster. More tests = quicker path to product-market fit. Learn more at Cofounder.AI.

Stage 4: Scale *(Chapter 6)*

You've got something people love—now it's time to supercharge it. This stage is about growing your user base, your team, and your revenue. It's also where many founders face the tough decision of whether to stay at the helm or bring in experienced operators.

- Get to cash-flow break-even (if possible) before you run out of capital; and/or

- Raise more capital (Series A or B round) to begin scaling your organization to capture market share (recommended).

- Build out your management team with operators (process-oriented management professionals).

- Develop sales and marketing processes with management so that new hires have a roadmap for success.

- Watch closely and monitor your company's growth and organizational metrics (for acceleration or decline).

- Ramp up PR for potential exit or further investment.

AI Scaling Trick: Implement AI-powered customer service to handle growth without ballooning costs. Learn more at Cofounder.AI.

Stage 5: Exit *(Chapter 7)*

The grand finale. Whether it's an acquisition or an IPO, this is where all your hard work pays off. But remember, oftentime the best exits are planned from the very beginning.

- Wait for suitors to come knocking: large industry incumbents will come if your success is known.

- Form strategic partnerships with potential acquirers to enhance their interest (optional).

- When one expresses significant interest, hire an investment bank to run a formal process to see if others are interested as well.

- Sell the company to the highest bidder with the best structured offer for you and your investors (cash is king).

- Take a very long vacation, put some money away for safekeeping, then start another company—it's in your blood.

Exit Strategy: You'll also learn the Reverse Liquidity Planning™ process (Chapter 7), a step-by-step process for engineering your exit from day one.

Thinking Like a Shareholder First

Some founders are born for the zero-to-one phase—taking an idea, sketching it out, and getting it off the runway. That's where I thrive. Over the years, I've come to realize that moving from concept to product is my favorite part of the startup process. It's the stage where I'm in my element, building teams, piecing together the plane, and making sure it gets airborne. Iterating is something I also enjoy, but it doesn't quite ignite the same spark. My sweet spot is assembling the pieces and pushing the startup into the skies. Sure, I can keep it cruising at altitude, but when it comes time to scale and hit a steady climb, I'm not always the one who should be in the cockpit. It took me years to fully understand this about myself. I'm a visionary, a product leader, and a builder, captivated by the startup process, or as Guy Kawasaki puts it, "The Art of the Start."

That doesn't mean I'm not the best person to guide the plane for the entire journey—because there is no substitute for founder DNA. However, as your startup moves through the Five Stages of Startup Success, you've got to keep asking yourself the hard question: "Am I the right person to lead through this phase of growth, or do I need to bring in someone better equipped?" Sometimes, the smartest play for both the company and your equity is stepping back into a chairman role and bringing in a new CEO to take the wheel for the long haul.

The AI Revolution: Funding's New Competitor

As we step into this new era of technology, raising capital might soon be overshadowed—or outright replaced—by leveraging AI. The game is changing, and it's changing fast.

Moving forward, every time you hit that familiar crossroad where raising money seems like the only option, pause. Ask yourself: *Could an AI tool solve or shrink the problem I'm trying to raise capital for?* Every time you think about raising money, ask yourself: Could AI solve this problem instead?

Here is how AI is reshaping the startup landscape:

1. **Customer Service**

    - *Enhanced:* 24/7 AI chatbots that respond to online chats and voice calls.

    - *Replaced:* Basic support tasks.

2. **Sales & Lead Generation**

    - *Enhanced:* AI-powered lead scoring and sales development reps.

    - *Replaced:* Early-stage prospecting.

3. **Marketing & Content Creation**

    - *Enhanced:* Personalized campaigns dynamically tailored to user personas.

    - *Replaced:* Basic content generation.

4. **Data Analysis**

    - *Enhanced:* Advanced pattern recognition providing insights for product improvements.

- *Replaced:* Basic report generation.

5. **Product Development**
   - *Enhanced:* Automated testing and AI-powered software engineers.
   - *Replaced:* Simple coding tasks.

6. **Hiring & HR**
   - *Enhanced:* AI resume screening and dispute counseling.
   - *Replaced:* Basic onboarding processes.

7. **Operations & Task Management**
   - *Enhanced:* Automated workflows and software-as-an-employee.
   - *Replaced:* Routine scheduling and management and entry level roles.

8. **Finance & Accounting**
   - *Enhanced:* Predictive cash flow analysis and financial presentations
   - *Replaced:* Basic bookkeeping

9. **Customer Relationship Management (CRM)**
   - *Enhanced:* Predictive customer needs and auto outreach
   - *Replaced:* Routine follow-ups

10. **Legal & Compliance**
    - *Enhanced:* Contract review assistance
    - *Replaced:* Standard document generation

Quick Action: For each area above, jot down one task in your startup that could be enhanced or replaced by AI. You might be surprised by how much you can automate!

AI isn't just a supplement—it's reshaping how startups function by slashing costs and boosting efficiency. By automating mundane tasks, uncovering actionable insights, and scaling marketing and support functions, AI lets founders focus on what really matters: innovation, growth, and building something that lasts.

The following chapters will walk you through the stages of startup success, laying out strategies for execution. At each stage, we'll explore practical ways to incorporate AI tools, prompts, and workflows to accelerate your progress.

Your AI-Powered Journey Starts Now

The startup world is changing at warp speed. With AI in your toolkit, you're not just building a company—you're pioneering the future of entrepreneurship. Are you ready to rewrite the rules?

Next up, we're diving deep into Stage 1: Conceptualize. Get ready to turn that napkin sketch into a fundable startup idea!

Remember, every time you see this 🐺 AI icon in this book, it's your cue to check out the CoFounder.AI platform for up-to-date AI tools, prompts and workflows tailored for each stage of your startup journey. Signup easily using the QR code below:

CHAPTER 3

Conceptualize (The Seed)

"Learn how to talk about money and don't be afraid to fail. Sometimes 'No' is the best blessing you can get."

— Nyakio Grieco, founder of Nyakio & cofounder of Thirteen Lune

The Art of The Start

Before you invest a single dollar or create anything tangible, let's dive into the critical process of conceptualization. This is your due diligence phase, your chance to determine if your idea is truly innovative or just another "me too" product that's missed its window of opportunity.

A word of caution: Vetting your idea is crucial. If it doesn't pass the *high-growth test,*[7] you'll face an uphill battle attracting capital and talent. Remember, building a startup is a different beast than building a small business. Let's get it right from the beginning.

Let me share a personal story. I remember being in middle school, dreaming of becoming an architect. That dream almost died the day someone told me, "You need to be good at math." Math was my enemy—until I flipped the script. I started telling myself, day after day, "I love math," like a personal mantra. And you know what? It worked. My grades improved, and I began excelling in a subject I once feared.

This experience taught me a valuable lesson: what you can conceive, you can achieve. The key is to bring what's in your mind into the physical world—write it down, visualize it, and create a roadmap. The more you commit your ideas to paper, the more real they become. That's when the magic starts happening. You'll begin to believe, and the more you build your confidence, the more others will believe as well.

Storytelling is key here—storytelling is the currency of both finance and fundraising. As an architecture student, I learned that people need to see something to believe in it. Words aren't always enough. There's an old Chinese proverb that captures this perfectly: "Tell me, and I'll forget; show me, and I may remember; involve me, and I will know." That's your mission in the conceptualization phase—don't just tell people about your idea, make them part of the story.

---

7. The **high-growth test** assesses a company's potential to rapidly scale revenue, expand market share, and capture a substantial customer base within a relatively short timeframe. VCs and sophisticated angel investors look for startups with the potential to deliver a 100x return within five-to-ten years. See: Understanding What's Fundable in Chapter 3 for more.

When you nail this process, you'll attract the right stakeholders—advisors, investors, cofounders—who see themselves as part of your vision. You're not just building a product; you're crafting a narrative that people want to be part of.

And here's the game-changer: with AI at your disposal, this process is now faster and more cost-effective than ever. It's like having a team of expert consultants working around the clock, helping you refine your concept and craft your story.

Conceptualizing your startup isn't just brainstorming—it's about equipping yourself with what you need to recruit talent, secure legal backing, and attract crucial seed investments. It's the foundation for your minimal lovable product (MLP), which we'll explore later. And with AI as your ally, this process is now faster and more budget-friendly than ever before.

Are you ready to execute and turn that seed of an idea into something real? Conceptualizing is your first step. Let's begin.

If You're Not Technical, Be Visual

Listen up, because this is important: In today's world, every company is a tech company. If you're not leveraging technology, you're practically begging to become obsolete. But what if you're not a coding whiz? No sweat. Here's my mantra: if you're not technical, be visual.

Here's a secret: I've founded tech companies, but I've never written a line of code. Shocking, right? But that hasn't stopped me from being a tech leader. My superpower? Staying on top of emerging tech and, more importantly, knowing how to visually communicate my vision.

Remember, a picture is worth a thousand words, but I'd argue a video is worth 10,000 lines of code. When you can tell your story visually, you're not just explaining your idea—you're making people experience it. That's how you get stakeholders to truly see your vision and jump on board.

Now, AI is making this visual storytelling even easier. But don't rush to the AI toolkit just yet. First, you need to nail down your narrative using my conceptualization process. Once you've got that solid foundation, I'll show you how to transform your story into a killer presentation, create eye-catching visuals, produce compelling videos, and even whip up podcast content—all using AI. It's like having a world-class creative team at your fingertips, ready to help you captivate the stakeholders who'll propel your startup forward.

So, ready to turn your idea into a visual masterpiece that'll have investors and talent lining up? Let's get started.

Conceptualization Process: From Zero to One

Here's my battle-tested roadmap for taking your idea from concept to reality. It has consistently delivered results, particularly in the development of software startups, but is equally applicable to creating physical products or even launching a venue.

Step 1: Vetting Your Idea (AKA, The Reality Check)

Before you quit your day job, let's put your idea through the wringer:

1. **Play Devil's Advocate**: List every reason why your idea might fail. Trust me, it's better to face these demons now than in a VCs office.
2. **Ride the Wave of Inflections**: In *Pattern Breakers: Why Some Start-Ups Change the Future*, Mike Maples Jr. emphasizes the

concept of "inflections" as key moments when external forces—such as technological shifts, regulatory changes, or societal behavior shifts.

3. Lyft is a good example. They caught the perfect wave when the iPhone 4S introduced GPS chips, enabling a peer-to-peer ridesharing service that wasn't possible before. What's your wave? What technological or societal shifts are making your idea possible now?

4. **Understand the Competition:** Who's already doing what you want to do? How can you do it better? If you don't have a really good answer to these questions and your competition has already raised significant funding, this should be your kill criteria.

5. **Talk to Real Humans:** Get out there and chat with potential customers. Would they actually pay for your solution? Brutal honesty is your best friend here. I have a saying, "it's trash, until it's cash." Potential customers will sometimes tell you that they will pay for your solution if it exists—but in reality, they won't. To combat this: See if you can get them to make a deposit before you've fully built it.

6. **Vitamin or Painkiller?:** Is your product nice to have or a must-have? Hint: Painkillers sell better than vitamins. When you remedy a customer's pain, they don't hesitate to pay.

7. **Product or Feature?:** Make sure you're not building a feature masquerading as a product. If it's just a feature, you may need to broaden your concept.

8. **Size Up Your Market:** VCs love big markets. Is yours big enough to get them excited? If your total addressable market (TAM) opportunity can't ultimately generate billions, it is too small of a market to excite investors.

Step 2: Understanding What's Fundable

To attract capital, you need to view your business idea through the lens of sophisticated investors—angel investors and venture capitalists (VCs). These aren't your average backers; they hear thousands of pitches a year, and they're looking for more than just a great idea. Often called "smart money," these investors bring expertise, market knowledge, and networks that can help take your startup to the next level. Feel free to review How Startup Finance Works: A Primer for New Founders in the glossary for definitions of financial terms.

Here is what makes angel investors and VCs take notice:

1. **Dream Team:** VCs invest in people first. Show them you've got the perfect mix of skills to execute your vision. The mix of technical, product, and sales expertise are critical. VCs aren't just investing in your product—they're investing in you and your team—even if your team is mostly AI.

2. **Massive Market:** Think billions, not millions. VCs want unicorns, not ponies. If your product solves a real, urgent problem and can grow into a billion-dollar market, you've got their attention. Skate to where the puck is going to be. Identify an emerging trend that will rapidly grow into a large market in the near future.

3. **Secret Sauce:** What makes your solution unique and hard to copy? Whether it's through innovative technology, a disruptive business model, or a *moat*[8] that's hard to replicate, VCs want to see something that sets you apart.

4. **Traction Talk:** Early customers or users? Flaunt those numbers. VCs love proof that you're onto something big. Nothing builds confidence like seeing the market respond to your product.

---

8. A **moat** refers to a sustainable competitive advantage that protects a company from competitors.

5. **Scalability Story:** Show how you'll turn your startup into a rocket ship, not just a speedboat. A clear path to market expansion and a scalable business model make you a more attractive bet.

6. **Money-Making Machine:** Have a clear plan for turning your cool idea into cold, hard cash. You've got to demonstrate that you're not just building something cool, but that you know how to turn it into a profitable venture. Remember this term: *Unit Economics*.[9]

7. **Exit Strategy:** Paint a picture of that juicy acquisition or IPO. VCs want to see the pot of gold at the end of the rainbow. Leverage the reverse liquidity planning process detailed in Chapter 7 to reverse engineer your path to liquidity.

8. **Perfect Timing:** Explain why now is the perfect moment for your startup to take off. VCs want to invest in startups that are positioned to ride the wave of emerging trends. If you can build a compelling narrative around the current market inflections—those shifts that make your solution timely and optimal—you'll stand out. Timing can make or break a startup, so get it right.

9. **Stretch that Dollar:** Prove you can do more with less. Capital efficiency is sexy in startup land. Demonstrate capital efficiency— show how you'll use funds and leverage AI to drive growth without waste. You're reading this book so you're off to a great start!

Remember, folks: Angel investors and VCs are looking for the next big thing. Show them you've got the team, the timing, and the tenacity to deliver significant 10-100x returns. Remember, you are competing for their dollars against other startups with 100x growth potential.

---

9. **Unit economics** refers to the direct revenues and costs associated with a single unit of a product or service, used to assess the profitability and scalability of a business model.

Step 3: Is It Go Time?

You've vetted your idea and it's looking fundable. Now, it's time for the million-dollar question: Are you the right person to bring this to life?

- **Founder-Market Fit:** The startup love story. Is this idea your soulmate? Does it keep you up at night, not because you're worried, but because you're excited? Does your background or past experience make you the ideal person to lead it? If you can't shut up about it and truly believe you're the one to make it happen, congratulations—you've got founder-market fit. It's go time!

- **Naming Your Brainchild:** 🦙 Give your idea a name that turns it from a fuzzy concept into something you can grab onto. A great name is like a birth certificate for your startup—it makes things official. Let AI be your creative partner: it's a pro at brainstorming names and crafting taglines.

- **Logo: Your Startup's Face to the World**. It's the visual DNA of your brand. It sets the tone for everything that follows. And once you have that logo in hand, your idea starts to feel more real, more concrete, more inevitable. You'll feel a stronger drive to build it, because now, it exists in some form. It has a face, now it's up to you to give it a body.

Step 4: Create Conceptual Illustrations— Your Idea, Visualized

Now it's time to give your idea a body—some visual weight—start sketching out what your product will look like and how it will function.

- **Wireframe It:** 🦙 Map out a basic blueprint of your product's layout and user flow. It doesn't need to be perfect or detailed—just enough to give structure to your vision. Show what goes where and how users will interact with each part, but without worrying yet about colors, fonts, or images. Your wireframe sketch will help you and your team align on the functionality and structure of your product before moving into detailed design and development.

Once you've laid the foundation by creating your wireframe, hand it over to a designer or AI to polish it up with more professional, conceptual renderings. The goal here is to make your vision feel real, not just to you, but to the people you'll soon be pitching.

- **Conceptual Renderings:** These are your product's first visual handshake. They help people understand what you're building and why it matters. They need to make people go, "Wow, I get it!" The clearer you make your vision, the easier it is for others to jump on your startup bandwagon.

    Pro tip: You only get one chance to make a first impression. So let AI or a professional user-interface (UI) designer do this work. You can find professionals on sites like Dribbble and Behance.

Remember, in the startup world, seeing is believing. So make your idea so visually compelling that investors and partners can't help but see the future you're building. Ready to turn that brilliant idea into eye candy? Let's go!

If you're eager to dive in, now is the perfect time to join the CoFounder.AI platform for the latest AI tools, prompts, and workflows designed specifically for this stage. Sign up at http://CoFounder.AI or scan the QR code below:

Step 5: Building Your Conceptual Deck— Your Startup's Debut

Alright, it's showtime! You've done the legwork, now let's package it all into a pitch deck that'll make investors take notice. This isn't just a presentation; it's your startup's debut to society.

Don't just show the facts—show and tell the story. Why is this the perfect time for your product? Why does this solution matter? Why are *you* the person to bring it to life? Investors don't just invest in products; they invest in stories, so craft a compelling one that weaves together your personal passion and founder-market fit. Remember, you don't have to be a great storyteller or writer, AI will do the heavy lifting for you.

Leverage Your Assets:

- Your product's catchy name
- That eye-catching logo (eat your heart out, Apple)
- Those slick conceptual renderings (better than any CGI).
- Real customer feedback (because who doesn't love a good testimonial?).
- Your total addressable market (show them the money!).

These aren't just slides; they're your ticket to the resources that you'll need to execute your vision. Use them wisely.

Craft a Narrative: 🐺 Don't just recite facts—levage AI as your creative partner to weave a tale that'd make Steven Spielberg jealous. Why is your product the hero the world needs right now? Why are you the chosen one to bring it to life? Remember, VCs aren't just investing in products; they're buying tickets to the greatest show on earth—your startup's journey.

Go-to-Market Strategy: Lay out a plan that's both scrappy and scalable. Show investors how you plan to get your product into customers' hands in a cost-effective way, while also highlighting the potential for growth. They want to see creativity, but also that you've thought through how to execute effectively.

This deck isn't just a pitch; it's your startup's origin story. Make it so compelling that investors will be fighting for a cameo. Ready to direct your startup's blockbuster? Lights, camera, disrupt!

Quick Action: Practice your pitch on AI before real people. Use a conversational AI to roleplay as an investor and get feedback. Learn more at Cofounder.AI.

Step 6: Sharing Your Vision— Laying A Foundation For Success

You've got your blockbuster pitch deck. Now it's time to pitch early supporters before expanding the deck to reflect their involvement. These are the people who'll help turn your vision from a cool presentation into the next big thing. Your opening pitches should be aimed at these key stakeholders:

- **Friends and Family:** Your first super fans. These are the folks who believe in you, even when your startup is just a glimmer in your eye. Their support—whether it's a check or a cheerleading session—is often the early fuel that you'll need to forge ahead.

- **Top Startup Law Firms:** Think of your legal team as the architects laying the foundation for your startup's skyscraper. Before you can build upward, you need a rock-solid base—this means officially incorporating your company and setting up a stock option plan for future employees. Without these critical first steps, your structure won't hold up when it's time to attract top talent or secure the investment needed to scale.

- **Bootstrapping tip:** If they believe in you and your vision, they'll agree to defer payment until you've secured funding—and may even open doors to investors along the way. As a startup founder, I've had the privilege of partnering with the following top startup firms at various stages of my journey: Cooley LLP, Wilson Sonsini (WSGR), Gunderson Dettmer, Perkins Coie, Fenwick & West, and Orrick

Step 7: Refine the Deck and Build Your Dream Team

Now that you have a little fuel and the right foundation in place. It's time to use it to recruit the people who'll help turn your vision from a cool presentation into the next big thing. This stage is crucial for your startup's growth and attractiveness to investors.

Pitch Deck 2.0: The Dynamic Presentation. Your deck should evolve as your startup does. As your team expands and your strategy develops, update your presentation accordingly. Keep it current, engaging, and compelling for potential investors.

Equity as Currency: Your Recruitment Tool. When cash is limited, equity becomes a powerful asset for attracting top talent.

- **The Optimal Allocation:** Reserve 10-15% of your startup's equity for a stock option pool. This allocation gives you flexibility in recruiting high-caliber individuals who believe in your vision.

- **Creating Invested Team Members:** Offering equity does more than compensate; it aligns your team's interests with the company's success. Team members with equity are often more committed and motivated to see the startup succeed.
- **Vesting:** A Protective Measure. Implement vesting schedules for equity distribution. As you learned in Chapter 2, vesting protects your company by ensuring that equity is earned over time, rewarding long-term commitment while safeguarding against early departures.

Are you prepared to use equity strategically and refine your pitch to its most persuasive form? This is your opportunity to build a formidable team and create a presentation that captivates investors. Let's transform your startup's potential into tangible progress by recruiting others. Cofounder- and advisor-matching services are available on the CoFounder.AI platform, along with other tips and resources for finding collaborators.

- **Cofounders and Consultants**: Assemble your A-Team. Start building your roster of cofounders or consultants with skills that complement yours. This isn't just about dividing the workload; it's about showing investors you're not a solo act, but a fully-equipped startup band ready to rock the market.
- **Advisors:** Your Startup's Jedi Council: Find your Yodas—advisors who've been there, done that, and lived to tell the tale. Their battle-tested wisdom can help you dodge rookie mistakes and open doors you didn't even know existed. Plus, having industry veterans on your side is like having a startup stamp of approval.
  - **AI advisors:** Learn how to leverage this book as an AI advisor by joining CoFounder.AI platform.

Remember, sharing your vision isn't just about pitching—it's about building relationships. These people aren't just stakeholders; they're the supporting cast in your startup's journey.

Step 8: Get Building and Get Funded (If You Need To)

If you haven't been building already, it's time to roll up your sleeves:

Sweat Equity: First things first, start building. You and your team need to put in some serious elbow grease. This sweat equity is your startup's initial rocket fuel—it gets you moving without burning through cash.

Need More Juice? Consider Pre-Seed Funding: If you need extra resources, leverage that updated deck. It's your golden ticket for raising pre-seed cash. A SAFE note (simple agreement for future equity) is the go-to method for startups at this stage. Your law firm can guide you through this process and platforms like LinkedIn and other networks can help you connect with potential investors. The CoFounder.AI platform includes resources to assist you with identifying the right law firm for your startup and AI tools that automate investor outreach.

Why are SAFEs popular? Using SAFE notes for early-stage fund raising enables you to skip the whole "what's your company worth?" headache when you're still figuring things out. Instead, investors get to invest cash now and sort out the details later when things are clearer.

The SAFE Advantage:

- Keeps your founder equity intact (for now)
- Gives investors some nice perks
- Cuts through the legal red tape
- No ticking clock or interest piling up

Basically, SAFEs let you focus on building your business without worrying about paying back loans or arguing over what your startup is worth before it has even launched.

Pro Tip for Approaching Investors: Don't go in guns blazing asking for cash. Instead, ask for their thoughts and feedback. Try something like, "Hey, I'm thinking about raising funds soon. Mind if I pick your brain on a few things?" This helps you build a relationship first.

Later, when you're ready to talk money, you can say, "Remember that chat we had? Your input was gold. We're raising pre-seed now, and I'd love for you to be in on this."

Remember, at this stage, investors are betting on you more than your idea. So focus on building that personal connection and showing them you've got what it takes to turn your vision into reality.

Step 9: Update and Expand

Team and Advisors: Your pitch deck isn't something you create once and forget—it's a living, breathing document that should evolve as your startup does. As you bring on new team members, advisors, or secure early investors, update your deck to reflect these milestones. This not only strengthens your credibility but also signals to future investors and stakeholders that your capacity to execute is growing.

By following this process, you'll lay the groundwork to transform your idea into a reality. From vetting the concept to building the product and securing funding, persistence is key. But with the right approach, you can set a solid foundation for startup success.

Step 10: Leverage AI Tools and Other Resources

If you try to tackle steps one through nine of the process without leveraging AI, you're leaving immense value on the table. The landscape of specialized AI tools, models, and apps is expanding at an astonishing pace, offering countless opportunities to accelerate and streamline your journey through the conceptualization process.

AI is evolving faster than ever, and to keep you ahead of the curve, we've built an online community and platform at CoFounder.AI to complement this book. Join the CoFounder.AI platform for the latest AI tools, prompts, and workflows designed specifically for this stage.

Sign up at http://CoFounder.AI or scan the QR code below:

CHAPTER 4

Launch!
(The Grape Stage)

"Incorporating AI from the launch phase can streamline product development cycles, leading to faster and more efficient innovation."

– Demis Hassabis, Co-Founder and CEO of DeepMind

From Seed to Grape: It's Go Time!

You've made it to the launch pad! Congratulations. You've conceptualized your idea and laid the foundation for making it a reality. You've got your first believers involved, maybe even some pre-seed cash in the bank and an early prototype. At this point, you've tested some product-market fit by having conversations with potential customers. However, everything up to this point is just theory.

It's time to make your idea real. Because ideas alone aren't worth much—execution is everything. In getting there, keep an open mind. I often tell entrepreneurs, "No business plan survives first contact with customers," and more often than not, I'm right.

Quick Action: Before we dive in, take a moment to visualize your launch. What does success look like? Jot down three key metrics you want to hit in your first month.

Where the Rubber Meets the Road

Your ability to introduce a product into the marketplace that gains traction will determine your success. So let's get real and bring your vision to life.

If you haven't built an early prototype of your product yet, don't worry—most resource-constrained founders complete the conceptualization phase without actually building the product. Now, it's time to find out how to get your product built. This is the first step toward launch.

You don't need to be a developer yourself, but someone on your team must have the technical chops to oversee the development process.

Who Will Build Your Product?

If you're not a developer (and let's face it, most of us aren't), your first mission is to find the tech talent to bring your vision to life. Here are your options:

1. Find a technical cofounder (the holy grail)
2. Hire developers (requires some technical oversight, but you're in control)
3. Outsource to an agency (quick, but pricey and less control)

Tip: Looking for a cofounder with technical chops, try using Y-Combinators (YC) Cofounder Matching Platform to find the perfect technical cofounder. Not ready for a full-on cofounder commitment? No worries. Hit up Upwork to hire remote developers.

Remember, tech-related products aren't one-and-done; they evolve. You need a team that can not only build but also iterate as your product and market demands shift.

Forget Viable, Make It Lovable

In this phase, your mission is to create a **minimal lovable product (MLP)**, execute your go-to-market strategy, and launch. Notice I said *lovable*, not *viable*. The minimum viable product (MVP) has been a buzzword for years, but in today's competitive landscape, viable just isn't enough. The MVP had its moment in the sun, but the bar has been raised. Customers today won't tolerate subpar products—they demand something they can love from the get-go.

Think about the apps you've downloaded—hundreds, perhaps—but how many do you use daily? Only a few make the cut. The ones that do aren't just liked; they're loved. They integrate seamlessly into your life, solving problems you didn't even realize were there, and once they've taken hold, you can't imagine living without them.

That's the goal. You're not aiming to create a product that's "good enough." You're aiming to build something that solves a pain point so well that your customers can't imagine life before it. When customers love your product, they'll use it religiously and, better yet, they'll tell everyone they know about it. This kind of organic, word-of-mouth growth is invaluable and can take your startup to heights no marketing budget can reach.

On the other hand, if customers only *like* your product, it becomes forgettable. They might use it occasionally, but it won't become part of their daily routine, and eventually, they'll drift away. That's churn. Churn is the enemy of growth. But when customers *love* your product, they stick around. They become loyal, and that's when you know you've built something special—a product that has the power to not only transform your company but to disrupt the market.

To build a transformative company, your mission is clear: find the customer segment that will fall in love with your product. Tailor it to their needs, and they'll fuel your growth far beyond what any marketing strategy could. Love creates loyalty, and loyalty drives exponential growth.

Quick Action: List three apps you use every day and can't live without. What makes them lovable? How can you incorporate those qualities into your product?

The Justin.tv to Twitch Transformation: A Love Story

> *The story of Justin.tv is one of those rare moments in tech where a pivot doesn't just save a company—it transforms it, creating an entirely new market in the process. It all started in 2007, when Justin Kan and his co-founders launched Justin.tv, a platform designed for live streaming. The original concept was simple: let people broadcast their lives to the internet, 24/7. In fact, Kan himself was the first "streamer," wearing a camera strapped to his head, streaming his day-to-day life for anyone to watch.*
>
> *The concept was novel, but it didn't quite catch on the way they'd hoped. While there was interest, the product lacked focus, and it*

wasn't clear which audience would truly fall in love with it. However, something interesting started to happen on the platform. Gamers began using Justin.tv to stream themselves playing video games, and they weren't just broadcasting—they were building communities. Viewers would tune in to watch, chat with the streamers, and engage with each other. For these gamers, streaming wasn't just entertainment—it was connection, competition, and culture.

The team realized they had stumbled onto something much bigger than a life-streaming platform. Gamers *loved* the product. They weren't casual users; they were passionate, dedicated, and vocal about what they wanted. The founders listened, and in 2011, they made a bold pivot, spinning off the gaming section of Justin.tv into a new platform—Twitch.

Twitch wasn't just a rebrand; it was a transformation. The platform zeroed in on the gaming community, tailoring the experience to their needs. Gamers could now easily stream themselves playing, while viewers could interact in real time. What had started as a side niche of Justin.tv quickly became a full-fledged phenomenon. The shift to Twitch didn't just lead to growth—it created an entirely new market: live streaming for gamers.

Twitch thrived, and its community exploded. Suddenly, millions of people around the world were watching others play video games, and it wasn't long before major brands, advertisers, and even professional eSports leagues started taking notice. Twitch had tapped into something unique—a passionate, engaged audience that didn't exist in this way before. The platform became the go-to destination for gaming content, and by 2014, Amazon saw the potential. In a landmark deal, Amazon acquired Twitch for nearly $1 billion, cementing its place as the leader in a new digital frontier.

The pivot from Justin.tv to Twitch wasn't just about surviving—it was about recognizing where the love was, where the passion was, and where the future was heading. By focusing on the gamers who loved the product, the founders didn't just build a successful company—they created an entirely new market that didn't exist before. That's the power of listening to your audience and being willing to adapt when the moment demands it.

Building Your MLP: Less is More (But Make It Awesome)

In **minimal lovable product (MLP)**, the emphasis is on *minimal*. Less is more. It sounds easy, but this is where the real challenge lies. Building a product that customers love, with fewer features, requires laser focus. It's about understanding what truly matters to your users and having the discipline to prioritize those core needs. Your product has to solve a problem so effectively, so elegantly, that users love it for its simplicity and power.

Here's how to build an MLP that will make users fall head over heels:

Must-Haves vs. Nice-to-Haves: Be ruthless. If it's not essential, it's out. Your launch version should consist only of the core features that users will find indispensable. Ask yourself: Does this feature directly address the problem? Is it vital for the product to function?

For instance, if you're building a ride-sharing app, features like GPS tracking and a ride request button are non-negotiable. Extras like user ratings or driver profiles can wait for future versions.

80/20 Rule: Launch with core features at 80% lovable. Once you release the MLP into the wild, real user feedback will help you perfect the last 20%.

The Onboarding Exception: This needs to be as close to perfect as possible—100% frictionless. No forms, no surveys. Just pure, instant gratification. Resist the temptation to gather data upfront. Don't ask for information before letting users engage with your product. You'll have plenty of time to collect data later, through *progressive engagement*.[10]

Instruction manuals? Those became obsolete long ago—especially in the software world. If your product makes users even think about looking for instructions, you're in trouble. Game over. Your product should be "self-evident," meaning its use is obvious without explanation. "Self-explanatory" is good, but self-evident is better. The faster your product feels natural to users, the faster they'll fall in love with it.

🦙 **AI Tool Alert:** Use AI-powered user experience tools to analyze and optimize your onboarding flow. The CoFounder.AI platform has curated options to get you started.

Steps to Building a MLP

Here's the process I've used to create an MLP that customers don't just like, but love. Follow these steps, and you'll be on your way to developing a product that resonates deeply with your audience while keeping your launch lean and efficient.

Establish a Minimal Feature Set

As a startup founder, establishing a minimal feature set means honing in on the core problem your product is solving for your target audience. Simplicity is your superpower. Here's how to approach this critical phase:

---

10. **Progressive engagement** is a design strategy in software development that gradually introduces users to features, presenting only core elements initially and revealing more advanced functions over time. This approach reduces overwhelm, simplifies onboarding, and encourages deeper user engagement as familiarity with the product grows.

- Step 1: Identify the Core Problem

    Start with a deep dive into the main issue your product aims to solve. Conduct customer interviews, market research, and competitor analysis to nail down the most urgent pain point. Your minimal feature set should laser-focus on offering a clear, direct solution to this problem—nothing more.

- Step 2: Prioritize Value

    List all the features you could include, then get ruthless. Prioritize based on how essential each feature is to solving the core problem and delivering value. Ask yourself: Does this feature directly address the problem? Is it vital for the product to function? If the answer is no, push it to a later version.

- Step 3: Start with a "Must-Have" Mindset

    Define what your product *must* have to operate in its simplest, most efficient form. Focus on features that:

    - Solve the primary user problem.
    - Offer a smooth, frictionless experience.
    - Clearly demonstrate your value proposition.

    For instance, if you're building a ride-sharing app, features like GPS tracking and a ride request button are non-negotiable. Extras like user ratings or driver profiles can wait for future versions.

- Step 4: Validate with Potential Customers

    Before writing a single line of code, test your assumptions with your target users. Share your wireframes or mockups, and gather feedback on the core features you plan to include. This step ensures you're building the right things and helps avoid wasting resources on unnecessary features.

- Step 5: Build Fast, Refine Often

Once you've nailed down your minimal feature set, build a fast, functional version of your product. Get it into the hands of real users as quickly as possible. Their feedback will be invaluable in guiding further development. Be ready to refine, improving or tweaking features based on real-world usage.

- Step 6: Avoid Feature Creep

Stay disciplined. Avoid the temptation to add "nice-to-have" features that don't directly solve the core problem. Feature creep can dilute your product's focus and slow down progress. In the beginning, keep your product laser-focused on delivering core value. Knowing what *not* to include is just as important as knowing what to build.

- Step 7: Do Things That Don't Scale

As you're building, keep scalability on your radar but don't be afraid to do things that don't scale if it improves the user experience. Once you've made your product loveable, you'll attract the resources you need to improve scalability. Focus on love above all else.

- Step 8: Set Clear Metrics for Success

Define what success looks like for your minimal lovable product. Are you measuring user adoption, engagement, retention, or something else? Setting clear metrics will help you gauge when your minimal feature set is hitting the mark—and when it's time to consider expanding.

The key to developing a minimal feature set is focusing on solving the most pressing problem for your users with the least number of features required. Stay lean, validate with your audience, and avoid complexity. This will keep your development fast, cost-effective, and focused on delivering maximum value.

To Stealth or to Splash? That is the Question

When it comes to launching, you've got two options:

1. **Stealth Mode:** More often than not, a quiet, soft launch is the smarter move. Perfect for gathering feedback and ironing out kinks, it avoids the possibility of a catastrophic, one-day failure that could ruin your company's future. Follow it up with a second, public launch with a more polished product.

2. **Big Splash:** Go big or go home. As an entrepreneur, you're not going to let fear stop you from going after what you believe in. So, if you're leaning toward making a big splash, then go all-in—alert the press, create a social media storm, host a launch event, and maybe even run a contest or giveaway.

    But know that a big, splashy launch can alert competitors, giving them an opportunity to undercut your product's success before you've gained enough momentum to compete. Further, the danger of disappointing customers is higher. A poor first impression can lead to bad reviews, negative press, and a serious loss of credibility.

Warning: A big splash can backfire. Just ask Humane. They launched the AI pin—a wearable device designed to replace many smartphone features. It had potential but lacked execution. They got publicly roasted by tech influencer

Marques Brownlee[11] to his 17 million subscribers. Brownlee's scathing review, calling the AI pin "the worst product I've ever reviewed," sent shockwaves through the tech community. Investor confidence evaporated, and as of this writing, the company is publicly up for sale.

Pro Tip: Raise capital before you launch. Sell the dream, not the data. Once you're live, you're married to your metrics.

By raising capital *before* the launch, you capitalize on anticipation, lock in better valuation terms, and keep more control over your startup's narrative. Plus, having capital in place before your product goes live extends your runway, allowing you more time to refine your product based on user feedback—giving you the breathing room needed to find product-market fit.

Countdown to Launch: Your Pre-Flight Checklist

1. **Assess Product Readiness:** Core features ready? Check. Major bugs squashed? Check. The product doesn't need to be perfect, but it should be stable and able to solve the main problem for users.

2. **Define Beta Goals:** What does success look like? Set clear metrics. Are you looking for user feedback, testing scalability, or validating certain features? Your goals will help you determine when the product is ready for beta users. Implement tools that track key metrics you want to measure.

3. **Time the Market:** Avoid holidays, major industry events, and competing product launches. If possible, align your beta launch

---

11. **Marques Brownlee**, also known as MKBHD, is a highly influential tech reviewer and YouTuber known for his in-depth, insightful reviews of consumer electronics, with over 19 million subscribers as of Noverber 2024.

with relevant industry events or conferences, where you can gain more attention from your target market.

4. **Coordinate Teams:** Everyone on the same page? This includes finalizing any last-minute product updates, preparing customer support for incoming feedback, and ensuring marketing has the right materials to promote the launch. Plan how you will handle incoming user feedback, bug reports, and feature requests. Make sure you have the resources to manage this input effectively post-launch.

5. **Buffer for Chaos:** Unexpected issues often arise during the final stages of product development. Build a time buffer into your schedule to account for any last-minute fixes or adjustments.

6. **Prep Beta Users:** Set expectations. Be transparent about the product's beta status. Let them know the product is still in development and actively seek their feedback to improve it. They're your partners in this journey.

7. **Marketing Timeline:** Build hype, but don't overpromise. Create buzz before launch with teasers on social media, email blasts, and influencer shoutouts to spark excitement and curiosity around your product. Plan to keep the momentum going after the beta launch with follow-up emails, user feedback sessions, and exclusive perks for your beta testers.

8. **Choose Your Date:** Be strategic. Pick a launch date that boosts your business goals—like syncing your beta release with a big funding announcement or an industry event to maximize attention and momentum. Also, make sure your A-team is all hands on deck.

9. **Feedback Loop:** Have a system ready to collect and act on user input. This will help you iterate on the product and prepare for a full release. Build flexibility into your timeline for making updates or fixes.

🦙 **AI Superpower:** Use AI-driven project management tools to keep all these moving parts in sync. It's like having a virtual project manager working 24/7. Learn more at CoFounder.AI.

Post-Launch: The Real Work Begins

Congrats, you've launched! But don't get too comfortable. The bulk of your journey—and your work—lies ahead. Here's what's next:

1. **Iterate Like Crazy:** Use that feedback loop to refine and improve. Scaling comes from mastering the small details first. Iterate your way toward the broader vision.

2. **Find Your Tribe:** When you spot users who love your product, double down on them.

3. **Go Deep, Not Wide:** Focus on delighting your core users before trying to appeal to everyone.

AI Boost: Don't forget to leverage the CoFounder.AI platform for cutting-edge AI tools tailored for each stage of your startup journey. Scan that QR code and supercharge your launch!

Remember, launching isn't the finish line—it's the starting gun. You've got a long, exciting race ahead. But with the right mindset, a lovable product, and AI as your co-pilot, you're set for an amazing journey.

If you haven't already, I highly encourage you to join the CoFounder.AI community and platform. Scan the QR code below to access our curated, constantly evolving AI resources that can help you execute more efficiently and stay ahead as you iterate and grow. The journey is just beginning.

Now go out there and launch something incredible!

CHAPTER 5

Iterate
(Nailing Product-Market Fit)

"Startups leveraging AI have a significant edge in understanding and anticipating market needs, leading to better product-market fit. Startups are about finding a path to scale, and the only way to do that is to build something people truly love."

—Andrew Ng, Co-Founder of Google Brain and Coursera

The Leaky Bucket Problem

Alright, future *unicorn*[12] builders, let's talk about the elephant in the room: product-market fit. Achieving product-market fit almost always requires

---

12. A **unicorn** is a privately held startup company valued at $1 billion or more. The term underscores the rarity of such high valuations, especially in early-stage companies, and often implies rapid growth, high investor interest, and substantial market potential.

iteration, and until you reach that sweet spot, scaling is impossible. Trying to scale without product-market fit is like pouring water into a leaky bucket. No matter how fast you bring in new customers, you'll keep losing the ones you have.

Reaching product-market fit isn't easy. In fact, it often takes two to three times longer than building the product itself. And here's where many founders go wrong: they think they've hit product-market fit when, in reality, they've only scratched the surface. True product-market fit is unmistakable.

You'll Know It When You See It

As Naval Ravikant, the sage of Silicon Valley, once said, "[True] product-market fit is like porn—you know it when you see it." When you hit that sweet spot:

- Word-of-mouth growth skyrockets
- Your customer retention soars, unit economics fall into place, and engagement metrics hit new highs
- Investors practically throw money at you

Until then? You're in the iteration trenches, my friend. Your focus should be a relentless cycle of building, measuring, learning, and iterating. Then, you repeat. And given how long this process can take, you need to raise enough capital upfront to ensure your team has the runway to get through this critical phase.

Quick Action: Grab a piece of paper and draw a bucket. Now, add some "leaks" and label them with reasons why customers might leave your product or rarely use it. This visual will be your reminder of what you're up against.

Fail Fast, Fail Cheap (But Keep Failing)

Remember Thomas Edison? He failed thousands of times before finally perfecting the lightbulb. When asked about his failures, he famously said, "I have not failed. I've just found 10,000 ways that won't work." Every failure teaches you something. Your job is to fail fast and cheap. Here's the game plan:

1. Build
2. Measure
3. Learn
4. Iterate
5. Repeat (until you're drowning in success)

Speed and efficiency are everything. The faster you can implement changes, test them, and gather feedback—without burning through your cash—the better your chances of finding that breakthrough that leads to product-market fit. Run as many experiments as you can, as quickly as you can, but keep costs low. This way, you'll maximize your learning without depleting your runway.

And here's the truth that every founder needs to hear: sometimes, even after all the iteration and effort, you'll need to pivot. This could be a minor adjustment or a complete overhaul, based on market shifts or early customer feedback. It happens more often than you'd think. Some of the biggest success stories, like Slack and Instagram, started out as completely different products before finding their true path.

The journey to product-market fit is one of the toughest stages, but it's also the most crucial. Keep iterating, keep learning, and be ready to pivot when necessary. Your breakthrough is just around the corner.

AI Hack: Use AI-powered analytics tools to speed up your measurement and learning phases. The faster you learn, the quicker you iterate. Learn more at CoFounder.AI.

The Pivot that Created Slack

Ever heard of a little company called Slack? Well, it wasn't always the communication giant we know today. Its origin story begins with Stewart Butterfield working on an entirely different product: a multiplayer online game called Glitch. Despite years of effort, Glitch failed to gain traction, and in 2012, Butterfield made the tough decision to shut it down.

But here's the twist: during the development, they built an internal messaging tool for team communication. They realized that this internal tool could solve a broader problem for other teams struggling with communication. That became Slack (searchable log of all conversation and knowledge). Slack quickly gained popularity for its ability to streamline workplace communication, reducing reliance on email. They pivoted from a failed game to a $27.7 billion acquisition by Salesforce.

Butterfield identified a real need, embraced flexibility, and turned a failed gaming project into one of the most successful workplace collaboration tools of the decade.

The lesson? Sometimes your biggest failure hides your greatest success.

Quick Action: List three potential "pivot points" for your startup. Where could you go if your current path doesn't pan out?

From Filters to Fortune: Instagram's Game-Changing Pivot

Instagram wasn't always about #influencers and dog photos. It started as Burbn, a location-based app with many features like check-ins, photo sharing, and planning meetups. It was trying to do… well, everything. It was too complex and didn't gain much traction.

But founders Kevin Systrom and Mike Krieger noticed users loved the photo-sharing feature. So they stripped everything else away, added some fancy filters, and boom—Instagram was born. Its simplicity and unique photo filters made it an instant success, gaining 25,000 users on day one and over 100 million within two years. In 2012, Facebook acquired Instagram for a cool $1 billion.

The takeaway? Listen to your users. They'll tell you what they love, even if it's not what you originally intended. Getting to simplicity isn't simple at all. But it may be your key to getting to product-market fit.

The Iteration Playbook: Your Step-by-Step Guide to Product-Market Fit

Achieving product-market fit is the most crucial milestone for any startup. It means that your product resonates strongly with your target market, leading to organic growth, customer retention, and business sustainability. Getting there takes constant fine-tuning—listening to customers, tracking key metrics, and sharpening both your product and go-to-market strategy.

Here's how it works—and how tools like *key performance indicators* (KPIs), *cohort analysis*, *net promoter score* (NPS), and *AI* can supercharge your path to product-market fit.

1. Monitor Like A Hawk

After launch, track everything. And I mean everything.

Key Metrics to Track:

- **Customer Acquisition Cost (CAC):** The cost of acquiring a new customer.
- **Retention Rate:** The percentage of customers who continue using your product over a defined period.
- **Churn Rate:** The percentage of customers who stop using your product after a certain time.
- **User Engagement:** How frequently users are interacting with your product's core features.
- **Lifetime Value (LTV):** The total revenue generated by a customer over the time they remain with your company.

This data provides a real-world perspective on what's working, what isn't, and where you need to focus your improvements.

Tools for Monitoring Metrics:

- **Cohort Analysis Tools:** Platforms like Mixpanel, Amplitude, and Google Analytics let you segment users by signup date to track engagement, retention, and churn. Comparing cohorts over time helps spot trends—like lower retention in recent users, which might signal issues with new features or onboarding.
- **Key Performance Indicators (KPIs):** Tracking KPIs keeps you focused on core goals. If retention is key, monitor metrics like monthly active users (MAUs) or daily active users (DAUs) to gauge customer engagement.

- **Net Promoter Score (NPS):** NPS gauges customer loyalty by asking how likely users are to recommend your product. Promoters (9-10) signal strong product-market fit, while detractors (0-6) offer insights on where to improve.

2. Refine Your Product

Continuously optimize user experience based on that mountain of data you just collected:

- **Enhance Core Features:** Make top-used features more intuitive. If users find a workflow clunky, streamline it to cut the friction.

- **Add Secondary Features:** After perfecting your core, introduce features that boost value without overwhelming users. Avoid 'feature bloat' to keep things simple and focused.

- **Test and Iterate:** Use early feedback to run small experiments on features or UI tweaks, and measure their impact on key metrics like retention and engagement. Rise and repeat.

  - **Leverage AI for Sentiment Analysis.** Tools like MonkeyLearn or Qualtrics can sift through user feedback faster than you can say "product-market fit." Automatically categorize common themes, complaints, or requests using responses from surveys, support tickets, or social media. This allows you to prioritize high-impact improvements.

  - **A/B Testing with AI.** AI tools automate A/B testing, quickly identifying which product variations boost user outcomes. Platforms like Optimizely test changes and suggest the best version for rollout.

3. Adjust Your Strategy (Flexibility is Key to Success)

As you refine your product, it's also essential to revisit your sales and marketing strategies based on data from user feedback and metrics. You may find that while the product improves, the way it's positioned in the market or sold may also need to evolve. Here is how to tune your strategy:

- **Play with Pricing: Find that Goldilocks Zone.** Feedback from your initial customers may reveal that your pricing doesn't align with their perceived value. Consider experimenting with different pricing models or offering tiered pricing plans to appeal to different customer segments.

- **Reassess Your Target Audience: You Might Be Surprised.** Cohort analysis might reveal your product clicks with a different audience than expected. If it resonates more with mid-market customers than small businesses, shift your marketing to target them.

- **Experiment with Sales Channels: Diversify!** If your launch focused on direct sales, try adding self-service or partnership channels based on early customer feedback and usage trends.

🦙 **AI Strategy Boost:** AI-driven predictive analytics tools can forecast user behavior and identify which leads are most likely to convert into paying customers, allowing your sales team to focus on high-probability opportunities.

4. Lather, Rinse, Repeat (Until You're Drowning in Success)

The key to success lies in repeating this iterative process—monitor, refine, adjust—until you achieve product-market fit. Reaching this milestone means continually learning from customers and refining the product to fit their needs perfectly. Keep this cycle going until:

- **Customers Stick Around Like Super Glue:** Customers renew subscriptions or repurchase your product at high rates. Engagement is strong, as is retention.

- **Your Net Promoter Score Is Through the Roof:** Lots of promoters and few detractors signal your customers are happy with the product.

- **You're Making More Money than You're Spending (Novel Concept, Right?):** Your unit economics are strong, meaning your customer acquisition cost (CAC) becomes lower than the customer lifetime value (LTV), ensuring profitable growth.

AI-Assisted Scaling Post Product-Market Fit:

- **AI for Customer Retention:** AI tools can help identify early signals of churn, allowing you to proactively engage users who are likely to leave and keep them engaged.

- **Automated Segmentation:** AI can automate customer segmentation, identifying which segments drive the most value and which need more attention, helping you refine your sales and product strategies as you scale.

The Story of MoviePass: Product-Market Fit Alone Isn't Enough

MoviePass is a cautionary tale of achieving product-market fit at the cost of poor unit economics. Founded in 2011 by Stacy Spikes and Hamet Watt, the company aimed to disrupt movie theater attendance with a subscription model. The service truly took off in 2017 when it slashed its price to $9.95 per month for unlimited movies, instantly attracting over 3 million subscribers.

While the offer resonated strongly with consumers, MoviePass's business model was fundamentally flawed. The company paid full price for every movie ticket its users redeemed, often spending far more than the $9.95 subscription fee it collected. MoviePass expected that, similar to gym memberships, many subscribers wouldn't fully use the service. They banked on the idea that a large portion of their customers would watch fewer movies than the average moviegoer, offsetting the cost of the heavy users who watched more than one movie per month. However, on average, users were watching 3 movies per month, costing MoviePass around $27 per user, leading to massive financial losses.

MoviePass didn't secure revenue-sharing deals with theaters, and its losses grew as more people signed up. Desperate, the company tried restricting movie choices, raising prices, and limiting usage, but these moves alienated customers and tarnished the brand.

Despite its initial success, MoviePass's poor unit economics—where the cost of serving each user exceeded revenue—led to its collapse. In 2019, the company shut down, showing that product-market fit alone is not enough; a sustainable financial model is critical for long-term success.

Not only can poor unit economics prevent your startup from scaling, even when you've achieved product-market fit, but I also learned the hard way that conflicting visions between cofounders can derail your path to success.

Why Progressly Failed to Scale: A Cautionary Tale

In 2014, I founded **Progressly** with the mission of transforming business processes into visual, repeatable workflows in the cloud—essentially "Pinterest for Processes." The idea came from my own need. As an entrepreneur with a background in architecture, I've always been a visual thinker. Whenever I executed a multi-step process, I would map it out horizontally on a whiteboard, using sticky notes to mark completed steps. This visual approach allowed me to think big while tracking progress in real-time.

I realized that this method could be digitized, creating a visual drag-and-drop interface where users could lay out multi-step processes as empty boxes connected in sequence. Once a step was completed, the user could drag their work into the box, which would be stored in the cloud, with the box changing to reflect a completed state. The user interface was slick and intuitive.

After showing the private beta version of the app to **Nick Candito**, a recent acquaintance who had just left a startup acquired by Salesforce, Nick made an offer that seemed too good to refuse. He promised that if I brought him on as a cofounder, he could guarantee we'd raise a Series A from a top VC. Fundraising had never been my strong suit, so I accepted. Besides, at the time, Silicon Valley's bro culture was in full swing, and Nick fit the mold perfectly.

Within six months, Nick delivered. Leveraging the early product and GTM strategy I developed, we quickly raised a $1.2 million seed round, followed by a $6 million Series A. I had little involvement in the fundraising process, remaining focused on product development and managing our offshore engineering team while Nick took the lead on raising capital. When we received the Series A term sheet, it was conditional that Nick would become CEO. I didn't mind—I've always seen myself as a shareholder first, so I moved into the role of Chairman, allowing Nick to manage the money he'd raised. In hindsight, this was a mistake.

Nick was a sales guy, not an experienced entrepreneur. I've always been more of a product visionary and go-to-market leader. Despite the successful fundraising, Progressly didn't have full product-market fit—only partial. Worse, Nick's priorities were building out an enterprise sales team and hiring a high-profile CTO, both of which drained cash and equity. Meanwhile, I pushed for us to focus resources on iterating the product to reach full product-market fit before scaling. This tension between us grew into a rift, and eventually, I was removed from the board. Since Nick had raised the money, he had closer relationships with our VCs, and they sided with him.

As I feared, within a year, it was clear we were burning through cash and a Series B financing was nowhere in sight. Fortunately, our patent, team, and vision attracted **Box** *(NYSE: Box), which acquired Progressly in 2018. Today, Progressly is the foundation for Box's workflow tool, Relay.*

In hindsight, the acquisition was a win, but had Nick and I been aligned on strategies, ethics and values as cofounders—and achieved full product-market fit before scaling—we could have unlocked far greater value.

Even with complementary skills, cofounders who lack alignment in values, respect, and trust are far more likely to derail the business and ultimately fail. Keep the Progressly story in mind when selecting a cofounder, and make sure to ask the cofounder interview questions outlined in Chapter 1.

AI Boost: Don't forget to leverage the CoFounder.AI platform for cutting-edge AI tools tailored for each stage of your startup journey. Scan that QR code and supercharge your iteration process!

Remember, the road to product-market fit is long and winding. But with persistence, data-driven decisions, and a willingness to pivot when needed, you'll get there. And when you do? That's when the real fun begins.

Now go forth and iterate like your startup's life depends on it. (Because, well, it does.)

CHAPTER 6

Scale
(A Grape, Grapefruit
& Beyond)

"The product that wins is the one that bridges customers to the future, not the one that requires a giant leap."

—Aaron Levie, Cofounder & CEO, Box

From Grape to Grapefruit: It's Growth Time!

Your startup has evolved from a tiny seed to a juicy grape, and now—thanks to product market fit, it's rapidly becoming a plum. Welcome to the scaling phase!

If your product hasn't gone viral yet—or even if it has—the most important factor is having a core group of people who genuinely love what you've built and are spreading the word. If you've got that, you're in a good position. Now is the time to ramp up marketing, keep improving the product, listen to customer feedback, and iterate. This feedback loop—where you refine, grow, and repeat—is your flywheel. Keep it spinning.

As you execute this process, you should also be growing into your valuation. Valuation, much like startup success, is as much art as it is science. Pre-launch, your valuation was likely based on factors like your team's quality, the scale of your vision, and your team's perceived ability to make that vision a reality. Essentially, pre-launch valuations come down to what "smart money" investors are willing to pay for a stake in your company based on its potential. You might think your startup is special, but unless investors see it that way, it won't affect your valuation—yet.

However, post-launch, everything changes. It's all about your growth metrics—a.k.a. traction. Traction is king, and it trumps everything. If you had trouble raising capital before, those days are over. Your traction is proof of product-market fit. When you've got solid sales, growing revenue, and clear momentum, sophisticated investors can now compare your company's trajectory to others. This establishes the basis for your new valuation. That's right, your grape is ready to be transformed into a larger fruit. This is a good time to raise growth capital to capture more market share.

Quick Action: Write down the size of your company based on your user base, revenue, or other metrics. Since you were a grape when you launched, what size fruit are you now? Draw it and visualize where your metrics need to be before you transform into an even bigger fruit.

Growing Into Your Valuation

Investors often use publicly traded companies as benchmarks to assess your startup's future potential. Let's say your startup is on track to generate $3 million in Annual Recurring Revenue (ARR) after a rapid climb from almost zero six months prior. Investors will take notice. Now that you're generating revenue, your valuation is tied to how much money you're making and, more importantly, how fast you're growing. If you're growing at 100% year-over-year, that signals a strong growth potential, which will lead to a significantly higher valuation than a company growing at 20% year-over-year. A slower growth rate might imply that your market is already becoming saturated. But if you're growing at 100% or more, your valuation could skyrocket, possibly hitting 10 times your Revenue Run Rate. That means if you're on track for $3 million in revenue, your startup could be valued at $30 million.

Growth isn't only about revenue, though—it's also about user acquisition, especially in the early stages. Companies like Facebook didn't focus on monetization in their early days; instead, they concentrated on scaling their user base. If you can become indispensable to your users, the money will follow. A platform with massive adoption always finds ways to monetize.

As your startup evolves, your valuation should rise along with it. If you raised your initial capital from friends and family, you may not have had a set valuation at the time (if you were savvy, you likely used a SAFE—simple agreement for future equity). But once your company matures and you start attracting more sophisticated investors, they'll set a formal valuation. For example, if new investors value your company at $10 million and invest $2 million, they'll expect roughly 20% of the company.

Remember, your early investors—those who supported you with a SAFE agreement—will also convert their investment into equity at this new $10 million valuation. Typically, they'll receive the same or a slightly better valuation (since they invested first) as the "smart money" investors who are now setting your company's value. This is a negotiation between you and your new investors, but SAFE notes will ensure that your earliest investors are fairly treated.

Whatever your valuation ends up being at this stage, your next objective is to leverage your new capital to scale the momentum you've built. If your company has grown from a seed to a grape during launch and now into a plum, the time has come to use your new capital, to transform it into a grapefruit by acquiring more customers.

Alternative Options: To Raise or Not to Raise?

You're at a crossroads. Do you: A) Bootstrap and aim for break-even or B) Raise capital and go for hypergrowth? Here's a quick pros and cons list:

Bootstrapping:

- *Pros:* Keep more equity, maintain control.
- *Cons:* Slower growth, risk getting outpaced by competitors.

Raising Capital:

- *Pros:* Fuel rapid growth, outpace competitors.
- *Cons:* Dilution, pressure from investors.

If you're bootstrapping your startup, make sure your revenue is at least covering your costs, and ideally, bringing in enough to reinvest. Even if you're crushing it, consider outside funding—especially if you've got competitors lurking. Here is some advice either way:

- **Don't Let Competitors Outrun You**: A competitor with more capital can outpace you in customer acquisition, leaving you in the dust. No direct rivals? You've got time to reinvest and grow. But stay alert—new players can enter anytime. If they gain traction, consider raising capital to keep the upper hand.

- **Raise When You Don't Need It:** At this stage, with proven demand, investors will likely offer better terms. Whether you're monetizing or building your user base with plans to monetize, the best time to raise is when you're not desperate for cash. Series B, C, or D rounds can take your early success to the next level.

- **Think Beyond Venture Capital**: Venture capital isn't your only option. Private equity (PE)[13] firms often seek a controlling stake but keep the founder involved, giving you a chance to offload some risk while staying in the game. PE often means a second shot at a major exit if they eventually take the company public or sell to a bigger player.

Invest for Success

Whatever strategy you choose for funding, you must know where to invest your money for maximum growth. So, where should you focus?

- **Boost Your Brand Buzz:** Amplify visibility with billboards, TV/radio ads, or social media. But don't overlook the power of PR—a dedicated press team can capture attention and tell your story.

---

13. **Private equity** (PE) refers to investment funds that buy and manage private companies, often with the goal of improving their financial performance and eventually selling them at a profit, either through an acquisition or by taking the company public.

- **PR for IPO Success:** If an IPO is in your future, strong PR is essential. It builds public awareness and attracts investor interest, positioning your company for success.

- **Attract Buyers, Don't Sell:** If a sale is your goal, focus on growth, not seeking buyers. You don't want to hang a "For Sale" sign on your business—that will only attract lowball offers from those assuming you're looking for an exit. Build momentum and use PR to catch the eye of industry leaders, ensuring you get offers worth your time.

Once you secure your new capital, it's time to scale up. If your startup has grown from a seed to a grape, now it's time to turn it into a plum, then a grapefruit.

Quick Action: Roleplay a quick pitch to an imaginary investor. What's your one-minute elevator pitch for why they should invest in your scaling efforts?

The Founder Mode Dilemma: To CEO or Not to CEO?

Time to look in the mirror, founders. Are you still the right person to lead this rocket ship? Here's a quick checklist:

- Do you thrive on chaos or crave process?

- Are you a visionary or an operator?

- Do you still wake up excited about your role?

If you answered "chaos," "visionary," and "hell yes," congratulations! You're still in founder mode. Founder mode describes a leadership style where the founder stays deeply involved in nearly every aspect of the business, even as the company begins to grow. In contrast to the more traditional *manager mode,* where executives delegate responsibilities to teams, founder mode emphasizes direct involvement, fast decision-making, and hands-on leadership.

Founders like Steve Jobs, Elon Musk, and Brian Chesky are classic examples of those who have thrived in founder mode. They kept a tight grip on their companies' vision, product development, and strategy, engaging with teams directly rather than following rigid hierarchical structures. This approach is marked by a high level of energy and urgency, as founders often have to pivot quickly, adapt strategies on the fly, and make bold choices without waiting for extensive analysis or approvals.

Founder mode means being involved in everything from product development to customer feedback, constantly iterating to find the best solutions and often working directly alongside the team to execute new ideas. It's about leading by example and inspiring the team through direct action.

But there are trade-offs. Critics argue that founder mode can lead to burnout, micromanagement, and a bottleneck in scaling. The challenge is finding a balance—keeping that founder-driven innovation alive while delegating enough to ensure smooth operations.

The Startup Team Makeover

Some people thrive in the chaos. They light up during brainstorming sessions, crushing real-time problem-solving. But when your startup shifts from scrappy to structured, those same folks might lose their spark.

Now is the time for a team reality check. Think of it like founder-market fit, but for scaling. Are you and your team the right ones to take this to the next level? If you've already realized you're not cut out to stay CEO long-term, it might be time to bring in growth pros who can level up your company.

Timing is everything. Don't bring in the "process pros" too early. These structure-lovers thrive when things are steady—but if your product-market fit isn't rock solid yet, they'll just get frustrated by the chaos. Let them build on a stable foundation, not in the middle of the uncertainty.

Quick Action: List three roles your startup needs to fill ASAP to scale effectively. Now, think about how AI could potentially fill (or assist with) each role.

Building the Machine: Growing Your Team for Hypergrowth

In the early days, your team can stay relatively flat. But as you scale, you'll need more oversight—particularly as you refine your business development and marketing strategies. This means you'll need managers, people who can keep the machine running efficiently. The bulk of the creative work is behind you; now, you need people who can run and grow a business.

- **Surviving the Scaling Grind:** Most startups never reach this stage, but if you're here, it's time to bring in an operations expert. A seasoned COO can refine processes and drive efficiency, especially one who has navigated hypergrowth before. They'll know how to avoid common pitfalls and keep things running smoothly.

- **Double Down on Customer Success:** Turning early customers into loyal advocates isn't enough now—you need a dedicated *customer success team* to fuel hypergrowth. They'll help keep customers engaged, happy, and coming back for more, transforming steady growth into explosive momentum.

- **Build Out Your All-Star Team:** Surround yourself with those who've seen it all—people with experience at other scaling startups and talent from larger companies who can fill critical skill gaps. Your mission now is customer loyalty; retaining happy customers demands a different approach than winning them over. Bring in experts who know the ins and outs of scaling customer retention.

Managing Emotions: The Startup Rollercoaster

As your company scales and its value grows, you might feel a rollercoaster of emotions. The fruits of your labor could pay off in a big way soon, which is exciting—but keep that excitement in check. Take a minute and appreciate what it took to get here. The decisions you make during this phase are critical, and acting rashly could derail everything.

In the early stages of conceptualization, you're excited because everything is still an idea—one that could change the world. You're painting a picture of your vision, setting hypotheses about how your product will solve a real pain point in the market. There's an air of anticipation, much like having a newborn baby.

When you launch, that concept becomes reality. Your company is no longer an idea; it's a real player in the marketplace, with actual customers. But after that initial buzz, the daily grind kicks in. Managing day-to-day operations isn't as straightforward or glamorous as you may have thought. You have customers to keep happy, and now the real work begins—that's the iteration phase.

Excitement can give way to exhaustion during iteration. You're not just trying to keep current customers happy—you're also working hard to get new ones while raising more money to fuel the next cycle of feedback, learning, and implementation.

Frustration can also creep in. You might have enough customers to stay afloat but not enough to truly scale. Your investors might start getting antsy. If the company can't scale, it risks becoming a lifestyle business—good enough to pay your salary and make payroll, but not the high-growth venture you envisioned. And that's not where most entrepreneurs want to be, especially if they've taken venture capital. VCs need a return, and a lifestyle business isn't going to deliver that.

I've been in this position before, and it's a tough place to be. Let me tell you about my journey as the solo founder of *CollectiveX*, later rebranded as *Groupsite.com*.

Groupsite: From High-Growth Startup to Lifestyle Business

In late 2005, fresh off the successful acquisition of ImageCafe and a three-year earnout as a VP at Network Solutions, the entrepreneur in me couldn't resist diving back into the startup world. Web 2.0 was hitting its stride, and it was an exciting time to build something new.

Web 2.0 was markedly different from the dot-com boom of the mid-1990s. Following the 2000 bust, it seemed like the internet had fizzled out. But by the mid 2000s, things were changing. High-speed internet was becoming widespread, open-source software made launching startups cheaper, and blogs were fueling word-of-mouth growth.

At this time, social networking was just emerging. MySpace and Friendster were dominant, Facebook was gaining traction on college campuses, and LinkedIn was just beginning. The closest thing to a group-focused social network was Yahoo Groups, which felt outdated as a simple listserv. I saw an opportunity: a platform that would allow anyone to create their own private online community for networking and collaboration. I called it **CollectiveX**, which later evolved into **Groupsite**.

Around the same time, Marc Andreessen and Gina Bianchini launched Ning, a similar concept. Ning raised significant venture capital, as did other emerging social business platforms like Yammer. Meanwhile, I was still based in Maryland, far from the Silicon Valley venture capital scene. Given my prior success with ImageCafe, I underestimated how important geographic proximity to Silicon Valley was for raising capital.

In 2006, venture investors on the East Coast weren't keen on backing consumer-facing startups that prioritized user growth over immediate revenue. As a result, I had to rely on local angel investors, raising money piecemeal—often in $50,000 increments—just in time to make payroll. From 2006 to 2008, I raised over $2 million this way, while competitors in Silicon Valley were securing millions in VC funding.

By 2009, Groupsite reached cash-flow break-even, but I was exhausted. We came close to being acquired by Yahoo as a replacement for Yahoo Groups, but the deal fell apart when Jerry Yang stepped down as CEO. While Groupsite was profitable, we weren't growing fast enough to attract the kind of capital needed to scale significantly. In contrast, Yammer was acquired by Microsoft for $1.8 billion, while Facebook and LinkedIn were skyrocketing.

Groupsite, meanwhile, became a lifestyle business—profitable but not at the scale we had hoped. If you're one of the angel investors who backed us, I want to say thank you. Groupsite is still operating today, keeping a small, dedicated team employed. In 2010, I stepped back into the role of Chairman and made the move I should've made earlier: I relocated to Palo Alto, the heart of Silicon Valley.

This is the reality of entrepreneurship. Sometimes you win big, sometimes you lose, and sometimes you land in between with a lifestyle business that doesn't return capital to investors. Every experience provides a lesson, and for me, Groupsite became the foundation for my next venture, **Progressly**—which you learned about in Chapter 5.

Zoom from Zero to IPO

One standout example of a venture-backed startup that successfully scaled to an IPO is Zoom Video Communications.

> Founded in 2011 by Eric Yuan, who had previously worked at WebEx, Zoom set out to create a video conferencing platform that was simpler, higher quality, and more reliable than existing solutions.
>
> Zoom's journey to an IPO was fueled by early venture capital investments, most notably from Sequoia Capital, which helped the company expand its product offering and customer base. Its innovative freemium model allowed Zoom to quickly gain traction, particularly in corporate environments where clear, stable video conferencing was critical. Zoom's emphasis on a frictionless user experience and strong customer satisfaction drove rapid adoption.
>
> In April 2019, Zoom went public, trading on the Nasdaq under the symbol ZM. The IPO was a resounding success—Zoom's stock surged 72% on its first day, reflecting high investor confidence in the company's growth trajectory and sound business fundamentals.

The company's success was further solidified during the COVID-19 pandemic, where it became an essential tool for businesses, schools, and families worldwide. Zoom's transition from a startup to a public company is a classic example of how strong venture backing, smart scaling, and the right market timing can lead to a successful IPO.

Zoom's story serves as a model for venture-backed startups with strong growth potential and a scalable product.

The AI Factor

Whether you're building your management team or leaning on AI tools to do the heavy lifting, the key is surrounding your business with the expertise and resources needed to grow effectively.

Join the CoFounder.AI community by scanning the QR code below or visiting https://CoFounder.AI to access an evolving wealth of AI tools and resources that can help you scale smarter, faster, and more efficiently.

CHAPTER 7

Exit
(Your Watermelon)

"When your startup is acquired, it's a celebration of your journey, an acknowledgment of your impact, and a promise of future potential."

—Mary Barra, CEO of General Motors

Building a startup that becomes an attractive acquisition target for a larger industry player is no small task. It's a testament to the incredible value you've created. When you receive an acquisition offer, whether you accept it or not, it's a moment worth celebrating. You've reached a significant milestone in your entrepreneurial journey. Even if you choose not to take the deal, the fact that your company has drawn interest from bigger players speaks volumes about what you've built, and you should take pride in that achievement.

Many entrepreneurs have achieved multiple successful exits, and they're often referred to as "serial entrepreneurs." I'm proud to be a member of **the multiple exit club** myself. As it stands, I'm currently the only Black American tech entrepreneur to have founded, scaled, and led two internet startups to acquisitions by publicly traded companies. If you've been following along, you're already familiar with parts of my journey. But despite how that sounds, I don't take pride in being "the only." This book is my way of changing that. My hope is that, with this book by your side, you'll be inspired and equipped to join the club.

Why Acquisitions Happen

Bigger companies often acquire startups because it's easier than competing. Large organizations tend to move slowly, especially when it comes to innovation. If your startup has a technology or product they need, it's often quicker and more cost-effective for them to buy you rather than build something similar.

There are also several other reasons for acquisitions. One is talent. If you've built a team of uniquely skilled individuals, the acquiring company may want those people on board. In cases like this, they may pursue an acquihire—a type of acquisition that's driven by the desire to bring in top talent rather than just products or technology.

Another motivation might be your patents, intellectual property, or other assets. If your startup holds something valuable, acquiring you means they can take advantage of these assets directly.

As your company grows and becomes a significant player in the market, larger companies may seek to acquire the entire business. They might not be just after your talent or technology anymore—they want the whole operation to eliminate competition and secure a strong position in your market. When acquisitions occur at this stage, your startup might even be well-positioned for an IPO.

That said, I won't dive too deeply into the IPO process here, as about 90% of venture-backed startups that exit do so through acquisition rather than going public. Plus, I haven't personally taken a company through an IPO, so it's not something I can speak to from direct experience. There are plenty of great resources out there if your startup is currently on the IPO trajectory.

However, I do have deep knowledge of the mergers and acquisitions (M&A) process—both as a startup founder who's been through multiple acquisitions and as an executive on the buy-side of a publicly traded tech company. This is where I can offer valuable insights not just on how to navigate an acquisition effectively, but steps that you can take to increase your startup's chances of ultimately being acquired.

The Reverse Liquidity Planning Process

What I'm about to share is something I started thinking about years ago, after the acquisition of ImageCafe. I call it **reverse liquidity planning**™ **(RLP)**. RLP is essentially reverse-engineering your path to liquidity—thinking about the endgame from the very start. It's a method that many serial entrepreneurs use instinctively. Individually, these steps might seem subtle, but when you connect the dots, they significantly increase your chances of a successful acquisition.

Ideally, the RLP process begins at the *conceptualize* stage. It forces you, as a founder, to consider potential exit scenarios before you've even set up your company. This not only demonstrates to early investors that you've thought through the exit strategy, but it also shows you have a clear roadmap for getting there. And let's not kid ourselves—investors are laser-focused on how you plan to return their capital, ideally with a 10x to 100x return.

Reverse Liquidity Planning™ serves as your compass on that journey.

Let's be clear, though: as a founder, your primary mission should always be to build a great company. Some will argue that thinking too much about acquisition possibilities early on might distract you from that mission. I don't see it that way. Strategic decisions in the early days should always have one eye on possible exit scenarios. However, none of that exit planning will matter if you can't execute on the first three stages of startup success—conceptualize, launch, and iterate.

By aligning your strategic decisions with the RLP process from the start, you'll set your startup on a path that maximizes the likelihood of a high-value acquisition for you and your stakeholders. It's about planning your future while staying laser-focused on execution today.

Here is how it's done:

Step 1: Refine Your Startup's Value Proposition

- Clearly define your target market and ensure your value proposition is concise and easily understood.
- Address a well-understood customer pain point with a solution that significantly boosts productivity and financial benefits.
- Identify the key business drivers in your market and the budget lines they influence most.
- Ensure there's no viable comparable alternative in the market.

Step 2: Perform Acquirer Analysis

- Identify the top three potential acquirers once you've gained traction.

- Assess how each potential acquirer will be affected by your startup positively (by purchasing) and negatively (by not purchasing).
- Understand each acquirer's financial position, their growth strategy (organic growth vs. acquisitions), and what they value most (IP, talent, etc.).
- Build relationships within these companies—identify key decision-makers and potential advocates through your network.
- Review their past acquisitions to gauge how founders and investors fared.
- Strategize about the best time to get on their radar (pre-Series A, Series B, etc.).

Step 3: Align Your Business Model

- Stay informed about market trends (consolidation, seasonality, etc.) and assess how much capital will be required to bring your product to market.
- Create a business model that could "plug into" an acquirer's existing infrastructure or distribution channels.
- Consider partnerships with potential acquirers to build relationships early, which can drive future acquisition interest.

Step 4: Align Your Identity and Communication

- Position your company as though it was tailor-made for the product line of potential acquirers.
- Develop a press strategy that positions your product as either a major opportunity or a threat to the acquirer.

- Coordinate a press and analyst tour around your product launch to increase visibility.

- Time your strategy so you appear on the radar of potential acquirers at the right moment.

Step 5: Align with Key Influencers

- Understand the VCs, angels, and business analysts who influence your industry.

- Choose a legal partner with connections to one or more potential acquirers.

- Build a board of advisors that includes individuals with strong ties to your target acquirers—such as investors, former company executives, entrepreneurs that have sold to your target acquirers and former corporate development personnel.

Now that AI is at our fingertips, the research and planning for reverse liquidity planning™ can be executed faster and more efficiently than ever before. If you haven't already, this is the perfect moment to join the CoFounder.AI community and platform. Simply scan the QR code below or visit https://Cofounder.AI to tap into an ever-evolving wealth of information, tools, and resources designed to accelerate your journey.

Types of Acquisitions

There are several ways an acquisition deal can be structured, but here's the golden rule: cash is king. If you can secure an all-cash deal, it gives you and your investors immediate liquidity, security, and certainty. Some companies may offer an all-stock deal instead, which essentially swaps your shares for theirs. If the acquiring company is publicly traded, you can cash out those shares after the deal closes—almost as good as an all-cash offer. However, if the acquiring company is private, you're banking on a future liquidity event, like an IPO or another acquisition, to get your return. It's a less favorable option because there's no immediate financial gain.

Startups typically encounter several types of acquisitions, depending on their stage, financial condition, and the acquiring company's goals. Here are the most common types:

1. Strategic Acquisition

> A larger company acquires a startup to gain access to its technology, talent, market, or simply to eliminate competition. In a strategic acquisition, the acquiring company usually integrates the startup into its existing operations for long-term synergies. A prime example of this is Google acquiring YouTube to dominate the online video space. Strategic acquisitions tend to focus on future growth and competitive positioning.

2. Acquihire

> In an acquihire, the main focus is on acquiring the startup's talent, not necessarily its product or technology. Often, the startup's existing products may be discontinued post-acquisition. This type of deal is common in tech, where highly skilled teams are

hard to come by. A well-known example is Facebook acquiring FriendFeed, primarily for its engineering team.

3. Tuck-In Acquisition

This occurs when a larger company purchases a smaller startup and integrates it seamlessly into its existing product line or technology suite. It's essentially a bolt-on acquisition that enhances or complements the acquiring company's current offerings. Think of it as adding a missing piece to an already established puzzle.

4. Asset Sale

In an asset sale, the acquiring company buys specific assets from the startup—like intellectual property, customer contracts, or technology—without taking on the entire company. This is often seen when a startup is in financial distress, allowing the acquirer to cherry-pick valuable assets without absorbing the liabilities.

5. IP Acquisition

Here, the focus is solely on the startup's intellectual property. The acquiring company might be interested in patents, trademarks, or proprietary technology to strengthen its own portfolio, even if the startup's overall product isn't of interest. It's a tactical move, particularly in industries where IP plays a critical role in competitive advantage.

6. Merger

Sometimes, a startup merges with another company of similar size or value to create a more competitive entity. This can be advantageous if both companies bring complementary technologies, markets, or resources to the table. The goal is to form a stronger, unified company that's better positioned for long-term success.

7. Roll-Up Acquisition

A roll-up acquisition occurs when a larger company acquires several smaller startups within the same market segment. This strategy allows the acquirer to consolidate the market, quickly increasing its market share and reducing competition. It's a common approach in industries that are ripe for consolidation.

8. Distressed Acquisition

In a distressed acquisition, the target startup is struggling financially or facing bankruptcy. The acquiring company swoops in to purchase it at a significantly lower valuation, often with the goal of restructuring and turning the company around. It's a high-risk, high-reward move, usually executed when the acquiring company sees long-term potential despite the startup's current challenges.

Each type of acquisition comes with its own set of motives and outcomes, shaped by the acquiring company's strategy and the startup's position in the market. Understanding these variations can help you navigate potential exits and maximize the value of your business when the time comes.

Deal Structure

Regardless of the type of acquisition, they can be structured a number of different ways. Example: A **hybrid acquisition** deal structure includes a mix of cash, stock, and possibly an earnout. An earnout means you stay on to run the business and must hit specific milestones to unlock the full acquisition price. This structure is common when the acquirer wants to ensure your company fulfills certain growth goals before fully committing.

This was the structure used when Network Solutions acquired ImageCafe in 1999. As the founder and CEO, I was required to stay on and lead the business for a three-year earn-out period, during which, we had to meet specific milestones to unlock the full acquisition price.

If your startup is backed by venture capital and running a high burn rate, you may face pressure to sell, especially if cash flow is tight. In such cases, you may have to look for buyers more aggressively, which can reduce your negotiating leverage. If you're burning cash and can't secure a Series B round, you might face dilution or be forced to raise at a lower valuation, which could push you to explore selling the company.

Even when the *burn rate*[14] is high, it's not always a red flag. As you've learned, oftentimes, startups deliberately operate at a loss to acquire more customers and drive usage, which can lead to a higher valuation. However, managing burn rate is key—whether you're negotiating a deal or trying to raise more capital, ensuring that your cash runway is stable will give you the flexibility to explore all your options.

Pro tip: As a founder, after the launch stage, every time I considered raising capital, I'd carefully calculate the dilution and potential loss of control that would result. Typically, if your startup is in a position to attract venture capital, it's also likely on the radar of potential acquirers. At this point, you owe it to yourself to do a "**net present value analysis.**" Ask yourself: "How much could I receive today if I sell the company at its current valuation, based on my current ownership stake, before raising another round?"

---

14. **Burn rate** is the rate at which a startup spends its cash reserves to cover operating expenses before generating positive cash flow.

It's important to understand that while each new funding round dilutes your ownership, it also strengthens the company's balance sheet, providing the capital necessary to grow the business from a small "grape" into a much larger "watermelon." Next, ask yourself: "Do I still have the passion, focus, and drive to grow the company further to ensure that my reduced ownership stake after this round ultimately becomes worth significantly more than my current ownership stake?" This reflection is essential to making informed decisions about the future.

Be Acquired or Go Public?

Acquisitions have become even more common in recent years. A study by Florian Ederer of Yale and Bruno Pellegrino of the University of Maryland shows that the percentage of venture-backed startups being acquired, rather than going public, has surged from 10% to 90% over the last three decades.

But while acquisitions are increasingly popular, they're not the right path for everyone. If you aim to scale your company and go public, you're betting on becoming the 800-pound gorilla in your industry.

Some of the world's biggest tech companies have turned down acquisition offers and thrived—Facebook (now known as Meta) famously rejected a $1 billion offer from Yahoo! in 2006, a decision that ultimately paid off with Meta's current valuation of over $1 trillion. Of course, other founders turned down big offers, hoping for even bigger success, only to see their companies fail.

Disruption is always around the corner, so whatever you've innovated today could become obsolete tomorrow. If your company is valued at $100 million, you never know when the market could shift. If you're startup is benefiting significantly from the hype generated by a *frothy market*,[15] be a little wary. Accepting a lucrative offer before it's too late can be a smart move—after all, no one ever went broke by selling too soon. Just ask anyone who turned down an acquisition offer right before a bubble burst.

---

15. A **frothy market** is a financial market characterized by rapid price increases driven by speculation and investor enthusiasm, often leading to inflated valuations that are disconnected from the underlying fundamentals.

CHAPTER 8

Seeing Around The Corner

"AI has been climbing the ladder of cognitive abilities for decades, and it now looks set to reach human-level performance across a very wide range of tasks within the next three years."

—Mustafa Suleyman, CEO of Microsoft AI

Are we on the brink of a new age of productivity and innovation, driven by unprecedented technological advancements? Absolutely. Have we faced something like this before? In fact, yes. Consider Colonial America, where 90% of jobs were agricultural. The Industrial Revolution shifted labor to mills and factories, and the Digital Age ushered in a service-based economy. Now, we're standing at the edge of what could be the most transformative era yet.

The reality is that many jobs as we know them will disappear. But if history has taught us anything, it's that humans are adaptable. Our larger brains have helped us survive and thrive through countless changes, and there's no reason to believe we won't do the same in the age of AI. How we adapt remains to be seen, but one thing is certain: the startup world is about to accelerate beyond anything we've ever experienced.

As an entrepreneur, don't resist the rise of AI—leverage it. Throughout this book, you've learned strategies to give you a competitive edge. In the coming years, success will belong to those who can adapt quickly to new technology, evolving customer behavior, and shifting economic landscapes. Why not be one of them?

Let's return to the cofounder dilemma. While AI can replicate some aspects of human interaction, it can't replace the emotional and strategic connection that human cofounders bring—at least not yet.

In 2024, we witnessed the rise of multimodal AI models that can interpret visual and auditory cues, assess emotions, and respond with empathy. Imagine AI that can detect if you're anxious or excited just by looking at your facial expression and react accordingly. Companies are even developing AI with an action quotient (AQ), a concept discussed by Mustafa Suleyman of DeepMind. AQ empowers AI to not only think and respond but also to act and complete tasks autonomously. As he put it during his TED Talk, we should start to view AI as a new digital species. I agree.

Robotics companies like *Figure* are pushing the boundaries by creating robots powered by Large Language Models (LLMs) that aren't just appliances but companions, much like the beloved C-3PO from Star Wars. These robots, with distinct personalities, could soon become everyday assistants. While it might sound like sci-fi, the future is closer than you think—it is my view that these innovations will arrive well before 2030.

Even as AI advances, human connection will remain vital. We are social creatures, and no technology can change that. Business is a team sport, and in the age of AI, the best teams will likely be a combination of human cofounders and AI agents working together. While we can't predict exactly what this future looks like, one thing is clear: AI will redefine the startup world. Instead of fearing it, embrace it—and let it drive your success beyond anything you could imagine.

Wrapping It Up

By now, you've been introduced to a wealth of information. You've learned a step-by-step process for turning your innovative idea from a seed into a watermelon. As we conclude with this final chapter, let's revisit some of the key takeaways.

First, the decision to bring in a cofounder should never be taken lightly. Before committing, have a semi-formal discussion about expectations, responsibilities, and how equity will be divided. **Cofounder relationships** are much like marriages—there will be disagreements. Establish a system for resolving conflicts early on to avoid stalling the business when opinions clash.

The most effective cofounder teams typically have **complementary skill sets**. One founder's strengths should balance the other's weaknesses. This dynamic ensures that all aspects of the business are covered.

When releasing your product, you have two launch strategies: a **soft launch** (private beta) or a big splashy launch. A soft launch limits the audience to a small target group, allowing you to gather feedback and iterate slowly. A big, public launch generates buzz but carries more risk—if things go wrong, the damage could be hard to recover from.

Focus on creating a **minimal lovable product (MLP)**, not just a minimum viable product. It's about building something that your best customers love and don't know how they survived without it before.

Product-market fit is non-negotiable. You must verify that your product has a place in the market and that people love it. This is a critical milestone, especially in the first stages: conceptualize, launch, and iterate. Any attempt to scale your startup before it has product-market fit, is like pouring water into a bucket filled with holes.

As founder, remember, **you are a shareholder first**. You will most likely be the largest individual shareholder in your startup for the foreseeable future. As such, as your startup grows, continue to assess your own role. Founders are often excellent in the early stages of a startup, but scaling requires a different set of skills, usually more process-driven. At some point, you might need to hand over the CEO role to someone better suited for that phase of growth, while you maintain significant influence via your board seat and a role with the company that continues to allow your talents to shine.

Start engineering your exit from the outset using the **reverse liquidity planning**™ process.

By understanding from day one during the conceptualization process which industry incumbents would benefit most for acquiring your startup and "reverse-engineering the path to liquidity" from there, you will not only be better able to effectuate and exit, but you will also impress early investors. Plan from the start how your company will eventually be acquired.

Above all, remember that **entrepreneurs are doers**. You're someone who embraces the unknown and pursues success. Now, with the knowledge of how to leverage AI to enhance each stage of your startup's journey, you have an edge.

While AI is rapidly evolving, human cofounders remain vital for now. There's no substitute for brainstorming with a human partner who shares your pain and joy along the journey. Though AI may eventually mimic human emotions, there's something irreplaceable about real human connection in business.

We're starting to shift from software as a service (SaaS) to **software as an employee (SaaE)**. AI can now handle tasks that used to require entire teams, whether it's customer support, sales outreach, or even financial analysis. In the near future, you'll be able to build a C-suite made up of AI experts—imagine a virtual CFO that reads every financial report in existence coupled with personality characteristics that you define.

The sweet spot for your startup might be a cofounding team where each founder manages a group of AI agents specialized in areas like finance, operations, and technology. Your cofounders might oversee AI-powered teams, rather than human employees.

In the end, whether you have human cofounders, AI, or both, the goal is the same: bring your idea to life and change the world. If you haven't already done so, if you are a new founder, or new to using AI, I recommend that you read **How Startup Finance Works** and **The AI Primer,** found in the glossary of this book.

Glossary

How Startup Finance Works: A Primer for New Founders

When building and financing a startup, founders will typically rely on two types of capital: debt and equity. Each has its own advantages and risks, and understanding both is crucial as you navigate the world of startup funding.

Debt vs. Equity

Debt Financing

Debt financing involves borrowing money that must be repaid with interest. Common examples include bank loans, lines of credit, or loans from private investors.

Pros:

- You don't have to give up ownership of your company. This allows you to retain full control over decision-making.
- Once the debt is repaid, the lender has no further claim on the business or its profits.

Cons:

- Debt typically requires a personal guarantee or collateral (like your house or business assets), which means you're personally on the hook if the business fails.

- Startups, especially in their early stages, are high-risk ventures, so taking on debt can be dangerous without a reliable revenue stream.

Equity Financing

Equity financing is when investors provide capital in exchange for owning a percentage of your business. In the startup world, this is common when raising money from venture capitalists (VCs).

Pros:
- No need to repay investors if the business doesn't succeed.
- Investors typically offer more than just money; they can provide strategic guidance, networks, and experience.

Cons:
- You give up a percentage of ownership and control of the business.
- The exit goal (how investors get their money back) often includes selling the company or going public through an IPO.

Note: High-risk startups in their early stages typically avoid traditional bank loans because they lack the steady revenue and collateral banks need to feel secure lending. Banks prefer businesses with proven track records, but startups operate in a world of uncertainty, focusing on growth and innovation, which inherently carries a lot of risk. Instead, startups raise capital by selling equity, giving investors ownership in the company in exchange for funding.

Startups also use convertible debt (defined below), such as bridge loans, which converts into equity down the line. This approach provides startups with the money they need without the pressure of immediate repayment, while also aligning investor interests with the company's long-term success.

Startup Funding Rounds & Financing Terms

When starting out, you'll encounter specific stages of funding and financial instruments designed for startups. Below are key terms and types of fundraising rounds to help you understand the startup financing landscape:

Convertible Loans (Convertible Notes)

Convertible debt is a hybrid between debt and equity. Investors lend money to the startup, which converts into equity during a future financing round. This allows investors to back the company early without immediately assigning a valuation.

Pros:

- Allows startups to raise money quickly without getting bogged down in valuation discussions.

- Investors receive equity at a discount once the startup raises its next *priced funding round*.[16]

SAFE Note (Simple Agreement for Future Equity)

A SAFE note allows investors to invest in your startup with the agreement that their investment will convert into equity during a future round of financing, usually at a slight discount and/or with a valuation cap.

---

16. A **priced round** refers to a startup financing round where the company's value (valuation) is formally determined, and new shares are issued at a specific price per share based on that valuation. Investors, in turn, receive equity in the company at this set price, which establishes the worth of their ownership stake. This contrasts with unpriced rounds, like SAFE notes or convertible notes, where the valuation and price per share are deferred until its next priced round.

Why SAFE Notes Are More Founder-Friendly than Convertible Notes

- **SAFE Notes**: SAFEs are more founder-friendly because they don't require repayment and don't dilute ownership until they convert into equity during a later funding round. This flexibility can give founders more control over their business in the early stages.

- **Convertible Loans**: Since convertible notes are loans, founders face the risk of needing to repay the loan if no subsequent funding round is raised before the maturity date. This creates a risk of diluting ownership early or burdening the business with debt.

Common Startup Funding Stages

1. **Pre-Seed:** The earliest stage of funding, often from friends, family, or angel investors. This capital helps get the company off the ground, usually before any product is launched.

2. **Seed Round:** After initial development, seed capital helps with product development, early marketing, and gaining traction. This round typically includes angel investors or seed-stage VCs.

3. **Series A:** Raised after you've proven product-market fit and shown some early success. Series A funding is focused on scaling the business, improving the product, and expanding your team.

4. **Series B:** Once the business has traction and needs to grow rapidly, Series B helps with expansion—whether it's entering new markets, ramping up sales, or acquiring new users.

5. **Series C & Beyond:** Later-stage funding rounds that focus on scaling globally, acquiring other companies, or preparing for an IPO. By this stage, the startup is often growing rapidly and requires large amounts of capital to fuel its operations.

Other Key Financial & Other Terms

Venture Capitalist (VC)

Venture capitalist (VC) are professional investors or investment firms that provide capital to early-stage or growth-stage startups in exchange for equity (ownership shares). VCs typically invest more money than angel investors and often focus on businesses with high growth potential. In addition to capital, VCs usually offer strategic guidance, industry expertise, and connections to help startups scale. They expect significant returns on their investments, often aiming for 10x to 100x returns through successful exits like IPOs or acquisitions.

Angel Investors

Angel Investors are individuals who invest personal funds into early-stage startups, usually in exchange for equity or convertible debt. Angel investors typically invest smaller amounts than VCs but often get involved at earlier stages of a company's development. While they also seek a return on their investment, angel investors may offer mentorship, advice, and industry connections to the startup, often acting as one of the first outside supporters of a business.

Smart Money

"Smart money" refers to investors who offer more than just financial backing. These are typically VCs or experienced angel investors who provide strategic guidance, industry connections, and mentorship to help your startup grow. They're also well-versed in leading funding rounds, helping to set a credible valuation that other investors will respect and align with.

Bridge Loans

A bridge loan is short-term financing used to "bridge" the gap between funding rounds or provide liquidity during a transitional phase. It's often used to keep the business running while preparing for the next significant round of financing. Bridge loans are structured as convertible notes or SAFE notes.

Liquidity

Liquidity refers to how easily you can convert an asset or investment into cash. In the context of startups, liquidity often refers to how easily investors can sell their shares—typically achieved during an acquisition or IPO.

Exit

An "exit" is how investors get a return on their investment, usually through a company being acquired (sold to another business) or going public via an IPO. Another term for "exit" is **liquidity event**, as it's the moment when investors and founders are finally compensated for their equity (ownership shares) in the company. The ultimate goal of startup investments is to achieve a high-value exit, where investors see a return of 10x to 100x on their original investment.

Pro Rata

Pro rata rights allow investors to maintain their ownership percentage in a company by giving them the option to invest in future funding rounds. This is important as it allows early investors to avoid dilution when the company raises more capital.

Run-Rate

Run-rate refers to a company's financial performance projected over a future period based on current data. It's typically used to estimate future revenue, profits, or costs by annualizing recent performance. For example, if a startup generates $1 million in revenue in one quarter, its annual run-rate would be $4 million, assuming similar performance continues for the next three quarters.

Run-rate is useful for assessing how a company might perform if its current growth trajectory remains steady, but it doesn't account for seasonal fluctuations, market changes, or unexpected events

Understanding how startup financing works—from debt and equity to various funding rounds and key terms—will help you navigate the world of venture capital and smart money. Whether you're bootstrapping or preparing for your first investment round, knowing these fundamentals will give you a clearer path toward building and scaling your company.

Risk Capital

Investors provide risk capital with the understanding that they could lose most, if not all, of their investment if the business fails. However, they are often motivated by the possibility of outsized returns, such as 10x or even 100x their original investment, especially if the startup experiences rapid growth or achieves a successful exit through an acquisition or IPO.

Risk capital is a common element in **venture capital** and **angel investing**, where investors fund businesses that have not yet proven themselves in the market but show significant growth potential. Unlike traditional investments, where stability is key, risk capital is focused on high-growth, innovative sectors that can offer exponential rewards in exchange for the greater risk involved.

Key Product Terms & Metrics

Business Model

A business model is a company's plan for how it will generate revenue and make a profit. It outlines the way a business creates, delivers, and captures value, explaining the core strategy behind how the company operates and sustains itself financially. A business model answers key questions such as:

- What product or service is being offered?
- Who is the target customer?
- How will the company generate revenue? (E.g., direct sales, subscriptions, licensing.)
- What are the key costs and expenses?
- What are the key resources and partnerships?

In short, the **business model** describes the broad framework of how a business functions.

Startups often adopt a variety of **revenue models** to monetize their products or services.

Here are some typical ones:

1. **Subscription Model:** Customers pay a recurring fee (monthly or annually) to access the startup's product or service. This is common in SaaS (software-as-a-service) companies like *Netflix*, *Spotify*, or *Slack*.

2. **Freemium Model**: The basic version of the product is offered for free, while premium features are accessible through paid upgrades. Companies like *Dropbox* and *LinkedIn* use this model.

3. **Advertising Model**: Revenue is generated by offering free content or services while displaying paid ads to users. *Google*, *Facebook*, and many media platforms rely on this model.

4. **Transaction/Commission Model:** The startup takes a percentage or flat fee for facilitating a transaction between buyers and sellers. Marketplaces like *eBay*, *Airbnb*, and *Uber* operate on this model.

5. **Affiliate Model**: The startup earns a commission by referring customers to another business or product. *Amazon's Affiliate Program* is a prominent example of this model.

6. **Licensing Model**: The startup licenses its technology, intellectual property, or content to other businesses for a fee. This is common in tech startups with patented innovations.

7. **E-commerce Model**: The startup sells products directly to consumers through an online platform. *Amazon*, *Warby Parker*, and *Casper* use this model.

8. **Data Monetization Model**: Companies collect and analyze user data, selling insights or access to other businesses. *Facebook* and *Google* use data monetization alongside other models like advertising.

Each startup might combine several of these models to diversify its revenue streams.

Unit Economics

Unit economics refers to the direct revenues and costs associated with a specific business model, measured on a "per unit" basis. In simpler terms, it's about understanding the profitability of your product or service on a per-unit level. A "unit" can be a single product, customer, transaction, or subscription—depending on the business model.

By analyzing unit economics, startups can determine whether the business is sustainable as it scales. The two key components are typically:

1. **Customer Acquisition Cost (CAC)**: How much it costs to acquire a customer, including marketing, sales, and any other expenses related to attracting new customers.

2. **Customer Lifetime Value (LTV):** The total revenue a company can expect to earn from a customer over the entire time they remain a customer.

In a healthy business, the **LTV** should be significantly higher than the **CAC**. This indicates that the company can afford to spend money to acquire customers because those customers will generate long-term profit.

Why Unit Economics Matters:

- **Sustainability:** It helps you understand whether your business can grow profitably.

- **Investor Confidence:** VCs and investors often analyze unit economics to see if your business model scales efficiently.

- **Strategic Decisions:** Knowing your unit economics allows you to make informed decisions about pricing, marketing spend, and scaling efforts.

In short, strong unit economics are critical to ensuring that growth leads to profitability, not just an increase in costs.

Cohort Analysis

Cohort analysis is a way to group users or customers based on shared characteristics or behaviors during a specific period, then track how these groups (or "cohorts") behave over time. It's a powerful tool for understanding how different groups of users interact with your product, which can help you make smarter decisions about improving your business.

For a startup founder, here's how it works:

Example:

Let's say you launch your product and start getting new users each week. You can create cohorts based on when users signed up (e.g., all users who signed up in Week 1 are one cohort, Week 2 are another cohort, etc.). By tracking these cohorts over time, you can see how their behavior changes—like how often they use your product, how long they stay active, or when they start dropping off (churn).

Why It's Helpful:

- **Measure Retention:** Cohort analysis helps you understand if your product is keeping users engaged. If you notice that users in one cohort are sticking around longer than others, you can look at what made that group different and try to replicate it.

- **Identify Churn:** It also helps you see when and why users stop using your product, giving you insights into where the product or onboarding process might need improvement.

- **Track Improvements:** If you make changes to your product, cohort analysis lets you see if those changes have made a difference. For example, you could compare the behavior of users who signed up before a new feature was added with those who signed up after.

In short, cohort analysis allows you to track user behavior over time, helping you understand what's working, what needs improvement, and how to make better decisions as you iterate your product.

The AI Primer

Understanding LLMs: The Backbone of Modern AI Applications

At the heart of today's AI advancements are large language models (LLMs). These models are trained on vast amounts of text data, allowing them to grasp patterns, context, and meaning to generate language that sounds human. By analyzing patterns and context across billions of sentences, they can predict and create text that mirrors natural conversation or writing.

Picture LLMs as AI systems with the knowledge of a lifetime's worth of reading—capable of answering questions, summarizing documents, holding conversations, and more.

What Are Multimodal Models?

While large language models lay the groundwork for AI language applications, multimodal models push the boundaries by processing and understanding multiple data types—such as text, images, audio, and video—all at once. This allows them to do more than handle language alone; they can analyze a photo, describe it in words, or combine image and text data to offer richer insights.

For example, OpenAI's GPT-4 is an LLM that powers many AI tools today, including Chat GPT. Meanwhile, DALL·E and MidJourney—other AI models—generate images from text descriptions. When combined, these multimodal models enable seamless interactions across different data types, creating a versatile foundation for AI applications.

Other notable multimodal models include Google's Gemini, Meta's LLaMA, and Anthropic's Claude.

How AI-powered Apps Are Built

What's an API and How Developers Use LLMs?

An API, or Application Programming Interface, acts as a bridge that enables different software programs to communicate. When it comes to using large language models for AI applications, developers can access the model's functions through an API without needing to create the model themselves. By sending a prompt to the API, they receive a response generated by the LLM.

Take OpenAI's GPT-4 API, for example: developers can send text input and get a natural, human-like response, making it easy to integrate LLMs into chatbots, automated content creation, customer service, and more, without needing in-depth AI knowledge.

So, when you interact with an AI-driven app, the API often connects the app with the LLM, enabling real-time responses and dynamic interactions.

What is Prompt Engineering?

Prompt engineering is the skill of designing precise inputs (prompts) to obtain optimal responses from a large language model. Think of it as providing clear directions to ensure the AI understands and delivers the desired outcome. Effective prompt engineering enables developers to make the most of LLMs, steering them to generate accurate, relevant, and helpful answers.

Best Practices for Prompt Engineering

1. **Be Specific:** The more precise and detailed your prompt, the better the response will be. For example, rather than saying, "Tell me about space," try, "Describe how black holes form in space."

2. **Provide Relevant Details:** If the model knows the context, it will provide more accurate answers. For example, if you're asking about a book, mention the title, author, and a brief description of what you're curious about.

3. **Iterate and Experiment:** If the first response isn't quite right, experiment with adjusting your wording—different phrasing can often yield better outcomes.

4. **Use Step-by-Step Instructions:** For complex requests, break them down for better responses. Instead of "Write an article," use "Write a 500-word article explaining how solar panels work."

The Role of AI and APIs in the Future of Innovation

By integrating LLMs, APIs, and prompt engineering, developers can create powerful applications that automate tasks like writing, customer service, and content generation—all fueled by AI in the background. With multimodal models, the possibilities expand further, enabling apps to work with not only text but also images, audio, and more.

Whether you're developing a cutting-edge app or using AI tools to enhance your business, understanding LLMs, APIs, and prompt engineering is essential to tapping into AI's full potential in the digital age.

Writing Good AI Prompts

As a startup founder, you can leverage LLMs like GPT-4 to role-play customer reactions to your product by crafting thoughtful prompts that simulate real-world scenarios. By embedding didactics (teaching methods) into these prompts, you can encourage the model to ask conversational questions that mimic a two-way dialogue, allowing for a more dynamic interaction.

Example Prompts for Role-Playing Customer Reactions:

1. **For a SaaS Productivity Tool:**

    Prompt: "Imagine you're a small business owner exploring a new productivity tool that promises to simplify task management and improve team collaboration. What features would catch your attention, and what questions would you have about integrating it into your existing workflow?"

    Didactic Elements: Instruct the LLM to role-play as a skeptical customer seeking more details. Use conversational questions like, "How does this tool integrate with the software I already use?" or "Will it actually cut down on the time my team spends on emails?" This approach fosters a back-and-forth dialogue, simulating a real customer discovery call.

2. **For a Health & Wellness App:**

    Prompt: "You're a fitness enthusiast who's been using a new app for personalized meal plans and workout routines. After a week of trying it out, what feedback would you provide, and what features would you be curious to explore further?"

Didactic Elements: Ask the LLM to provide a balanced response, offering both praise and constructive feedback, and to include questions such as, "How do you adapt meal plans for specific dietary needs?" or "Can I link my fitness tracker to this app?" This method refines product positioning and brings key user needs into focus.

3. **For an E-Commerce Platform:**

   Prompt: "Picture yourself as an online shopper discovering an e-commerce site that claims to provide quicker delivery and exclusive discounts. How would you react initially, and what questions might you have to learn more about what's offered?"

   Didactic Elements: Encourage the LLM to act as a customer by asking questions such as, "What guarantees faster shipping on your platform?" or "Can you tell me more about the exclusive deals offered?" This approach helps identify possible concerns and points that may require further clarification.

Using Didactics for Conversational Questions:

To make the conversation more engaging, didactic prompts should:

- **Encourage Follow-Up Questions:** Guide the LLM to ask follow-up questions based on prior responses, creating a more natural dialogue flow. For example, "Faster shipping sounds great, but how does your return policy work?"

- **Probe for Deeper Understanding:** Instruct the LLM to respond as a curious customer interested in learning more about the product. For example, "That sounds helpful, but can you explain how it benefits small businesses like mine?"

- **Highlight Concerns or Curiosities:** Encourage the LLM to bring attention to common hesitations or questions. For example, "This feature seems interesting, but I'm worried about the learning curve. How easy is it to onboard my team?" This approach helps to reveal areas where users may need reassurance or additional support, offering insights into how to highlight the product's ease of use and accessibility.

This method helps you understand how a target customer might react, what features need more explanation, and where potential friction points are.

Learn more about prompt engineering for accelerating each of the Five Stages of Startup Success by scanning the QR code below or visiting https://Cofounder.AI. You'll gain access to an ever-updating wealth of information:

AI Bias and Its Origins

Biases in AI models, including large language models (LLMs), can arise from multiple factors:

1. **Training Data:** AI models are trained on massive datasets collected from sources like the internet, books, and media, all of which reflect the biases of their human creators. These biases—whether social, racial, gender-related, or political—are often embedded in the content, leading the AI to potentially absorb and replicate these prejudices.

2. **Historical Data:** When training data contains historical inequalities or prejudices, the AI may unintentionally carry these forward, resulting in biased outputs. For example, if the data over-represents certain demographics or viewpoints, the AI may produce responses that reflect this imbalance.

3. **Imbalance in Data Representation:** AI models can also become biased when trained on data that over-represents one group or viewpoint while under-representing others. This imbalance means that the AI may perform better for the groups represented more prominently in the training data while producing less accurate results for under-represented groups. With facial recognition, the training data under-represented people of color, leading to significant challenges in identifying faces with darker skin tones. This lack of inclusivity created critical failures in real-world scenarios where accurate performance was essential. Comprehensive bias testing or proper auditing of their training data can prevent these potential problems.

4. **Model Architecture:** Bias in AI can also arise from the structure and design of the model itself, which influences how it processes and prioritizes information. For instance, certain architectures may place more emphasis on specific features over others, potentially amplifying biases if those features are unequally distributed across different demographic groups. When developers set priorities or tune parameters to optimize for specific outcomes, they may inadvertently reinforce these biases, particularly if the training goals reflect assumptions that aren't universally applicable.

Guardrails with RAG and Context Windows:

To reduce biases and enhance the accuracy of AI-generated responses, two key techniques are gaining importance: retrieval-augmented generation (RAG) and expanded context windows.

Retrieval-Augmented Generation (RAG):

RAG integrates a large language model with a document retrieval system, enabling the AI to access and use relevant, trusted information from external sources instead of relying only on pre-trained knowledge, which may be limited or biased.

How it helps with bias: By retrieving specific information from reliable sources in real time, RAG reduces the likelihood of the AI relying solely on biased or outdated pre-trained knowledge. This allows for more informed and balanced outputs, as the AI draws from the most current and relevant data.

Context Windows:

AI models use context windows to manage the amount of text they consider while processing and generating responses. These windows define how much surrounding information the AI can retain, allowing it to create outputs based on a broader and more cohesive set of details. For instance, you can include whole documents in the prompt, enabling the AI to use the content within as context for more informed responses.

How it helps with bias: Larger context windows enable the AI to process more nuanced information, which helps mitigate the risk of producing biased outputs based on a narrow view. For example, in a discussion of gender roles, a larger context window allows the AI to consider multiple perspectives in the conversation, reducing the risk of a biased or stereotypical response.

Together, RAG and context windows help put "guardrails" in place for AI systems. RAG ensures the AI has access to updated and accurate information, while context windows ensure that the AI maintains the integrity and depth of the conversation. These tools are becoming crucial for reducing bias, ensuring factual accuracy, and improving user trust in AI-generated content.